# If I'm Healed By His STRIPES, Then Why Do I Still hURt?

### Rebecca Maisenbacher

the Covenant center publishing house

If I'm Healed by His Stripes, Then Why Do I Still Hurt?
by Rebecca Maisenbacher
Published by Covenant Publishing House
26 Lake Wire Drive
PO Box 524
Lakeland, Fl. 33802-0524
www.covenantpublishinghouse.com

Editing, design and layout by Dominion Marketing Communications, Inc.: www.dominionmarcomm.com
Cover art by Virginia Celoria
Cover design by Amey Celoria

Printed in the United States of America

ISBN: 978-0-615-60259-2
SECOND EDITION
Library of Congress Control Number: 2012933913

# Contents

# Dedication & Acknowledgements

This book is dedicated to Jesus, who has always walked with me on my journey of self-discovery. He is my best friend, my counselor, my truth, my health, provision, strength, revelation, peace, joy and life. His unconditional love has continued to bring peace to my heart. Jesus, you are the healer of my soul's diseases.

Thank you Mom and Dad for your love, tireless work and sacrifice, as you always loved me, provided for me, encouraged and desired the best for me. You have given me an amazing heritage and history. I am very grateful to God for placing me in your care and in this very special family He chose just for me.

Thank you to my husband, Richard, who has been not only my lover, but also my friend and companion; a faithful counselor and encourager to me in this journey of life. Your continued patience and endurance in running this race with me has been comforting. Your support and love have been a foundation for me to grow and stand upon. God chose perfectly as He placed us together as one.

To my son Zachary and his wife Melissa, thank you for the years of prayer and patience with the many challenges of living with a family member battling chronic pain. Your continuous flow of love, understanding and forgiveness has been a healing balm to my soul. Your hugs have often raised my endorphins and brought happiness and refreshing to me. You and your precious children, Elijah and Noah, have brought absolute joy. I have been blessed beyond measure to be granted the privilege of having you in my life.

I am grateful for you dear brothers, Barry and Shannon, who have also walked with me on this amazing journey called life. Thank you for the memories of us all as family, of childhood games, victories and defeats, life experiences and relationships that are held dear in my heart. Shannon, thank you for sharing your professional insight as I researched some of the more technical aspects of this book. Never could I have chosen two more brilliant, gentle, kind and compassionate brothers as you.

Heather, Amey, Melissa, and Kathy, I thank you for your friendship and support as well as your editing and technical skills. Your insight and encouragement truly held up my arms in this venture.

Lidy, Jeri, and Anita, thank you for daily watching over our TCC family with your skilled and loving ways, while I "jumped ship" to finish this odyssey.

And to my Covenant Center family, thank you for your love, trust and support as you have allowed me to grow and be healed and transformed in a safe and nurturing place where God's love and healing abounds.

# Introduction

Dear Reader, this book you now hold in your hands is simply a story of my personal quest for healing and truth. I do not presume to be an expert on healing. I do not profess to have all the answers to the century old question, "Why isn't everyone healed?" Like you, I have only my personal journey and testimony to share. I hope my experiences will bring comfort and encouragement to those who find themselves on a quest for healing and truth, as well as those who may have at some time in their journey doubted the love and faithfulness of God.

When teaching or writing on the topic of healing, there is always the concern that the information will be used to control or condemn others, point the finger, develop a formula or process it in some legalistic way. That is not my intention. God takes us from glory to glory, revelation to revelation, as He reveals His diversity and the various ways He heals. Jesus was moved with compassion and extended healing in many ways. May we learn from our Lord's many beautiful examples of healing and extend His love and encouragement to others during their challenges and trials.

If you have endured any kind of suffering in your life, I am simply inviting you to take a walk with me as I share my personal journey regarding healing. Most healings I have experienced or observed have involved a process requiring more than one intervention; often involving medicine and counsel, as well as revelation, repentance and forgiveness. As we journey together through this book, I hope you will see your Father's greatness and faithfulness, and how much He loves you. It is my prayer that you will be encouraged, enlightened and healed by His power as He reveals special truths to you personally.

At the end of each chapter you will find a list of personal

unhealthy thoughts and unbiblical paradigms I entertained for much of my life. The unbiblical beliefs or thoughts often hindered me from experiencing joy, healing and life. I permitted these thoughts to steal precious time from me, my family, and my friends. They were destiny robbers. They often were the root of sickness and disease that would manifest in my body.

Also included at the end of each chapter, you will find Scriptures and Biblical truths which brought clarity, life and hope to me. As I studied and meditated on God's Word, I began to see more clearly the unhealthy thoughts and negativity I had chosen to entertain. When Jesus was led into the wilderness in Matthew chapter four, He was our example of how to combat unbiblical beliefs. He responded to the temptations and challenges of the enemy by declaring the Word of God and stating, "It is written." Jesus demonstrated how Scripture counteracts the deceptive, divisive, condemning, accusing, lying and exalting thoughts we entertain in our mind as truth.

As I began to recognize the unbiblical thoughts assaulting my mind, declaring and meditating on Scripture and God's promises became an integral part of my healing process. My thoughts and perceptions slowly began to change. I noticed health in my body began to return as well. It became apparent that my diseased soul was affecting my physical body.

Jesus is the Healer. He is Jehovah-Rapha (Rophe). I came to understand He heals the diseases of our soul as well as the diseases of our body. As you study and declare these Scriptures over your life, may they bring you healing, clarity, hope, and peace as they light the path of your personal journey of healing, revelation and transformation.

Every day is new and full of experiences and challenges we can choose to embrace or suppress. Holy Spirit is able to search our hearts and reveal hidden beliefs or motivations that may hinder us from experiencing joy, freedom and healing in life. If you sense confusion, grief, disappointment, anger, despair, or other negative reactions to circumstances in your life, allow yourself time to be quiet as you begin to search for the underlying root of the pain you are experiencing. Our emotions are a good barometer to examine when we respond negatively to challenges or when we are unaware of hidden pain or unbiblical beliefs.

I have personally found journaling to be helpful in exposing my thoughts and revealing truth. Talk with God as you read and write. Give yourself permission to discuss any pain or frustrations you are feeling with Him. He is eager and waiting for you to come to Him. Seek the counsel and guidance of professionals and friends as you begin to face any unresolved conflict within you. God tells us in Isaiah 45:3, "I will give you the treasures of darkness, and hidden riches of secret places that you may know that it is I, the Lord, the God of Israel who calls you by your name." It is my prayer that you will find the treasures of darkness God has stored up for you and revelation from heaven will begin to turn your sorrow and pain into joy and dancing.

"Search me, O God, and know my heart; Try me, and know my anxious thoughts; And see if there be any hurtful way in me, And lead me in the way everlasting" (Psalm 139:23-24).

Let's continue together to "press toward the mark for the prize of the high calling of God in Christ Jesus" (Philippians 3:14), being strengthened and encouraged by His love. His unfailing love will guide us, as we travel our personal journey toward revelation, health, joy, wholeness, restoration, and His resurrection life: "For we know that all things work together for good to those who love God, to those who are called according to His purpose. For whom He foreknew, He also predestined to become conformed to the image of His Son, that He might be the first-born among many brethren."

## Notes

God's names and reference to His name and Scriptures are capitalized purposely to give honor to Him and His Word.

## Disclaimer

The information and suggestions in this book are only intended to serve as encouragement and to give guidelines to those who continue to search for healing in their bodies and minds, as well as their spiritual journey. It is always recommended that you discuss any symptoms, medical conditions, diagnosis, use of medications, as well as herbs or other nutritional supplements, therapies or exercise with your doctor.

# 1
# THE ACCIDENT

When I was small life seemed so simple. It was easy to love, to trust, to hope, and to believe the world was my oyster and I could do anything if I just put my mind to it. Our minds receive simple facts and we believe what we are told or what we experience is truth. But as we grow up, life begins to engrave its marks on us and we begin to change. Whether through people or encounters, we begin to feel the need to somehow keep our happiness and dreams alive. We want to feel secure and productive, so we may develop conflicting beliefs in our attempt to stay connected or current with society and its ever changing values. Or we may simply make choices in the tsunamis of life to merely take care of ourselves and stay alive. Every human at birth embarks upon an amazing journey of learning to live life. Our mind, soul, spirit, and body travel along with us as we experience and learn about our world. They help us to continually process information around us as we develop skills, beliefs, perceptions and life goals. When a trauma or unexpected loss occurs, our beliefs and goals are challenged. As we try to process painful events we can become confused or disoriented. We may feel out of control. Painful seasons of life can either strengthen us or they can destroy us.

It was 1975, on a dark and isolated road through the corn fields of northern Ohio, when my life took a severe turn. Hit by a drunken driver in a serious head-on crash, I lay unconscious with my friend Angie, as the paramedics arrived. We were finishing our last class of graduate study. I was excited to be completing my master's degree. It had been three grueling years of classes, tests, papers and long nights. The driver had passed a semi-trailer on a double yellow-lined curve. He was intoxicated. I remember seeing the bright lights coming toward us, looking over at Angie, and then...darkness. The semi-trailer driver had witnessed the accident and called for emergency assistance. We were taken to the nearest hospital. The next thing I remember was someone shaking me awake. The foggy-headed feeling in my head made me unable to focus. Everything was fuzzy. As I looked straight up into the ceiling lights of the hospital, a blurred shadow appeared. As I strained to look more intently, I could see the outline of a man with a State Trooper's hat on his head. He introduced himself as an Ohio State Trooper. He leaned over and whispered in my ear that I was a very lucky young woman; that the severity of the accident should have taken my life. Then, he was gone. I closed my eyes once more to complete darkness.

I was hospitalized for a few days for tests and observation. As I lay in the hospital bed recuperating, the vision of the State Trooper's shadow hovering over me returned and what he whispered resonated in my ears. I remembered just minutes before the crash I had sensed the need to put on my seatbelt. They were not worn regularly then by drivers or passengers. I realized the sweet gentle voice of the Spirit had reminded me of my "pact" with my husband to always wear our seatbelts when we were apart.

After being released with only aches and pain, vertigo, tinnitus, and a mild concussion but miraculously no internal bleeding, cuts or scrapes; I attempted to resume completing the last class of my degree. It was also the end of the school year, and as a Speech-Language Pathologist, I needed to write up my reports and education plans on each of my students. The pain in my body continued along with the vertigo, muscle spasms and a mental lethargy. Back pain, leg pain, neck pain, shoulder pain, hip pain.... relentless pain was an everyday experience. At times the pain was constant, chronic and debilitating; exhausting, frustrating and never ceasing. It was difficult to think clearly or to multi-task as before the accident. I would become overwhelmed with my work, household chores and any mental tasks required of me. Riding in a car as well as hearing the sound of semi's driving by would trigger anxiety and panic within me. I would constantly tell my husband how to drive trying to control my environment to feel safe. Post Traumatic Stress Syndrome and Traumatic Brain Injury were not familiar terms to me or my doctors at this time. Within months, we sold our house and I resigned from my job.

## Searching For Relief

The pain I was now living with, that I feared and cursed, was the very pain that would force me onto a future path and search for healing. Desiring relief but feeling weak left me confused and overwhelmed. Over the years I visited numerous doctors and specialists, took pain medication prescriptions, endured physical therapy and consulted nutritionists. I visited chiropractic clinics and received physical therapy and massage treatments. Various exercise programs with stretching and aerobics were endured, but the pain never completely ceased. Even my weekly trips for counseling left me sitting in my car after my sessions, crying out and asking, "*What is wrong with me God?*"

Being in pain 24 hours a day touched every aspect of my life. Days and weeks turned into months and years of relentless pain. Grocery shopping and house cleaning were arduous tasks. Keeping my job to help pay our bills was my main focus. It took all my energy to get through the day and when I would finally arrive home, I would crash. Trying to have friends over or make family visits was also exhausting. When I did experience mild relief and I attempted to step out and enjoy an activity or exercise, within days I would find my body ravaged in pain again. The pain was like a ball and chain; when I would try to step forward, it would pull me back. Fear began to grow in my heart. The world was passing me by. I observed everyone else living their lives while mine seemed to stand still. I was sitting on the sidelines while others seemed to be enjoying life – experiencing life. *What was wrong with me? Would I ever be normal again?*

# A Fresh Start

We moved to Dayton, Ohio in 1978. I was excited to have a fresh start. However within one year, we were struggling financially and stressed without permanent employment. Richard and my youngest brother, Shannon, who was living with us, had been hired as commission salesmen for a water treatment company. This meant we only paid our bills when one of them made a sale. We all began to feel the stress of living month to month wondering if we would be able to meet our mortgage and car debt.

One evening Shannon came home unusually excited and joyful from a long evening appointment. It was late so we thought he had made a big sale. However, he told us of a kind and gentle family he had met during his sales presentation. He had been drawn to the calm and serene presence they exhibited. Before the night was over they had presented their story to Shannon of how they came to know Jesus as their Savior. They shared that their peace and contentment came from Him. I actually do not remember if they purchased a water softener that evening, but I can say Shannon accepted Christ that night and he immediately came home and shared the hopeful message of Christ with Richard and me.

Just days before in my anger and frustration, I told Richard he had better get down on his knees and ask God to help us. I accepted the Lord as a small child, but that night I began to realize I didn't know Him. I knew about God, but I didn't have a relationship with Him. I knew the Bible stories and that I should pray every day to Him. Even though I had grown up in the church world, I never understood that it was best for a couple to be equally yoked before they married. In other words, I had married a nice and kind man who went to church periodically, but he had never accepted Christ. My husband had been living without revelation of God's truth in his life and I had lived with little knowledge of God's ways and precepts. However, that very night in Dayton, Ohio, Richard gave his life to Christ and I followed by rededicating myself to Him. I asked God to forgive me for ignoring Him and going my own way.

How glorious we all felt. Our days were now filled with a great sense of peace and joy. Love and excitement seemed to be radiating through us. We wanted to learn more about Jesus. Negative situations in our lives began to turn around. Jobs began to appear and we were able to pay our bills. My body was pain free. The colors of the world seemed brighter. Hope had been birthed in our hearts. Stress was released and such glorious warmth and anticipation filled my heart again. I returned home to God with my husband by my side.

If you have made choices in your life that have harmed you or others, it is never too late to ask God to help change you and give you hope and a future. Scripture states that God has plans for you. He has plans that are not to harm you, but to give you a future and hope (Jeremiah 29:11). In John 3:16, we are told that "God so loved the world, *(that's you and me)* that He gave His only begotten Son, that whoever believes in Him will not perish but have eternal life." We are able to stand on God's future and hope in challenging times. Eternal hope lies in Jesus and God's promise of living forever with Him. If you have experienced deep hurts and pain in your life, Jesus is the ultimate healer and counselor. He will guide you in your life so pain and fear do not consume you anymore. Maybe you would like to ask Him to help you right now?

---

*"Dear Jesus, I am tired of fighting life's battles on my own. I don't know how to do life. I am asking You now to come and live with me, to be my Savior and Lord, as well as my Father and Friend. Please forgive me for all the poor choices I have made and the pain I have caused You, others, and myself. Please help me. Renew my mind and purify my heart. Help me become new. I now receive You. I receive Your love, Your forgiveness, Your strength, Your mind, joy, and Your resurrection life."*

---

Maybe you have known God for a long time and somewhere in your life you decided like me to just try things on your own. Like the prodigal son, we thought life with God was just not working out or fitting into our dreams so we decided to leave home. Maybe your life has resulted in famine and loss, where the things you held so dear have now vanished. You may think you could never return to God because you feel unworthy or unlovable. Beloved, it is never too late to return to God. All of heaven celebrates when a beloved son or daughter returns. In Luke, chapter 15, the prodigal son's father went running to him, embracing and kissing him with love and compassion. When we return to God, His love is poured over us as a cleansing, healing balm. He rejoices and celebrates as He reminds us, "My child, you have always been with me, and all that is mine is yours" (Luke 15:32). Consider returning to God's unconditional love and acceptance with this prayer:

*"God, I have wandered away from You and Your statutes. I have missed the mark and caused heaven and earth pain. I know I am unworthy to be called Your son/daughter, but I want to come home. I'm tired of doing things my own way. I've lost everything. I don't know what to do anymore. I now receive Your forgiveness, Father, and Your love. Please help me now. Renew my mind and create in me a pure heart and a right spirit. I return to Your covenant of peace. Thank you Father."*

## Pain, Pain, Go Away

Quickly we found a wonderful community of believers. We wanted to grow and to understand what we had all experienced. As the years passed, we were privileged to sit under many great pastors who shared wonderful truths. It was a very exciting time in our lives. We worked, we studied and we attended church regularly. Our son was born in 1980 and we experienced such hope. We taught in the church preschool, sang in the choir, taught various study courses and completed Bible School.

After a Sunday service in 1984, my husband and I were walking down a long, quiet corridor of the church. It had been a refreshing and peaceful gathering and most everyone had left the building for the day. As we slowly continued walking, an outline of a lady appeared. It seemed odd that she was coming into the building and heading toward us. I remember commenting earlier to my husband that it was unusual for us to be the last ones to leave. As we met in the middle of the long, quiet hallway, she quickly said *"Hello"* and politely asked if she could share something on her heart. We said *"Of course,"* and she began to explain. *"I have been praying for you and sensing that God is asking you to trust Him. You are going on a journey with Him and He is going to reveal to you many dark things, hidden things within your heart. He says to trust Him, trust Him."* This was a rather ominous message that appeared to be a word of prophecy, although at that time I was basically unaware of prophecy or any gifts of the Spirit. The only thing I knew at that moment was the stirring in my stomach. My inner man or "knower" told me what she was saying might have some truth, but my mind was racing trying to figure out what she meant. *"What dark things? I can't have any dark things in me; I have Christ living in me."* Stunned and somewhat bewildered we returned home. I wrote her short message down and tucked it away, choosing to forget the event, although the memory was now etched into my mind forever.

Periodically the pain in my body would reappear. It would return with a vengeance. Muscle spasms would throb in my neck, back and shoulders. Sometimes the pain seemed almost more than I could bear. The visits would become more frequent to chiropractors, medical doctors, orthopedists, massage therapist, and acupuncture practitioners. The search continued for anything that would make the pain go away. Prescription drugs prescribed, but they made me groggy and dull minded, so I would try to live without them. I would read and meditate on Scripture trusting that *"I was healed by Christ's stripes,"* but the healing wouldn't appear. Through the 1980's I attended healing classes, deliverance courses, and various other seminars. Sometimes I would be told I didn't have enough faith; so I would try harder to have enough faith to be more acceptable to God so He would heal me. I repented of everything I could ever remember in my life that I had done or said or thought. The harder I tried to become acceptable for healing, the more stress and pain I would feel.

"God, I guess you haven't been able to forgive me for the abortion." A year before my car accident I had undergone an abortion, which I will discuss in more detail later. I repented and asked forgiveness, but when challenges appeared I sometimes wondered if I was still being punished for the decision. My mind battled with what I read in the Bible, what I heard from the pulpit, and what my husband, family, and friends would say. I seemed to be hearing conflicting messages. "You are not worthy. No, you have sinned. Yes, you are worthy. You have enough faith. No, you just don't have enough faith. Healing is for all, but God doesn't choose to heal everyone." It was confusing. Did God desire to heal me? Would I ever be healed? No one seemed to be able to find the source of the pain in my body and no one knew how to help.

Through all the years of searching for a root cause the experts were never able to give me a clear diagnosis. I was diagnosed with fibromyalgia, chronic fatigue, nerve damage, inner ear problems, post traumatic stress, severe depression and anxiety and various other things. Was it neurological, a chemical imbalance, misalignment of my spine, a head injury, shoulder injury, or poor nutrition? One dear doctor, after reviewing my x-rays, blood work, and various other tests declared to me, "Honey, go home and be happy, this is just all in your head." As I left his office, I became angry and indignant. "How could this all be in my head? I am in pain....I can hardly walk or sit. I can't sleep at night. He doesn't understand what I am going through. He doesn't understand the pain. I am just fine emotionally. I'm a college graduate. I have won awards and titles. How dare he say this is all in my head!" Of course, years later into my healing journey I would discover this doctor's words were more prophetic than he or I realized.

My husband and son endured days, weeks, months and years

of long trips to doctors with me. The pain I was experiencing was stealing their lives as well as mine. I felt guilty and ashamed. *Why couldn't I be like other wives and mothers? Why wasn't I strong and able to do things with my family? "Dear God where are You? Please, help me! This has been happening for over 20 years. What is wrong with me? Why can't the doctors help me? What am I doing wrong? Why can't You heal me?"*

## Negative Beliefs

God loves others but I am unlovable.
If I do enough nice things for people maybe God will heal me.
If I'm busy and performing for God He will be good to me and bless me.
If I work really hard maybe He will like me more and help me.

## Scriptural Truths

God loves unconditionally.
God's desire is for none to perish and all to have everlasting life.
Working harder or performing for God will never make Him love me more than He already does right now.
Reading and meditating on Scriptures helps reveal unbiblical beliefs in my heart and soul.
Truth will always find me when I ask for it and am willing to acknowledge it.

## Scripture Meditations: "It is written...."

Deuteronomy 31:6 — "Be strong and courageous, do not be afraid or tremble at them, for the Lord your God is the one who goes with you. He will not fail you or forsake you."

Psalm 94:14 — "For the Lord will not abandon His people, nor will He forsake His inheritance."

Isaiah 41:17 — "When the afflicted and needy are seeking water, but there is none, and their tongue is parched with thirst; I, the Lord, will answer them Myself, As the God of Israel I will not forsake them."

John 3:16 — "For God so loved the world that He gave His only begotten Son, that whoever believes in Him should not perish, but have everlasting life."

## Reflections...

# 2
# MUSTARD SEED FAITH

If you have ever been seriously ill or challenged by prolonged pain you are very aware how we continually hope for a miracle touch that will bring some kind of relief and divine intervention. It is easy to feel like we have lost hope or faith when long battles and challenges begin to bring weariness and sadness. This place of reflection and self-examination can be treacherous if we allow our thoughts to lead us to a place of loneliness and despair.

Through the 1980's and 1990's, we continued in our commitment to attend church regularly. It was not uncommon to see me going forward for prayer. Whenever there was a call for prayer I was there, hoping for the glorious moment when the pain would vanish. There were some in our congregation who looked at me with eyes of compassion; but there were others who look at me with suspicion, as if to say, *"What sin have you committed that has kept you from being healed?"* I began to feel like a leper. Saints would sometimes encourage me with *"You just don't have enough faith!"* That would really lift my spirit. Week after week going forward for healing and prayer sometimes resulted in a few days of relief, but the pain would always return. I found myself spiraling downward to the depth of shame and despair crying out to God to *"just take my life."* I knew I had become a burden to my husband and family. The medical bills and doctor visits were our recreational time together. This pain and agony was eating away our lives. After years and years of feeling debilitated, I didn't know if I could take it anymore. I felt I would never have enough faith. I was tired of suffering. I just wanted it all to end.

Years into my journey I would discover I did indeed have enough faith – just as you do dear friend. Romans 12:3b states that "...God has allotted to each a measure of faith." All we need is the mustard seed faith God has already measured to us to believe. And even in those moments when our faith may seem to waiver or we are just too weak to stand, a simple request for Him to help us is all that is required. *"Jesus, help me"* has sometimes been the only phrase I could speak. God has always arrived to love me, encourage me and give me strength to endure, and He will do the same for you. For many years I lived without being able to recognize the truth in my life and why I had to endure such pain and loss. I submitted to the deception that God had left me, as I listened to Job's comforters confronting me and telling me I did not have enough faith. How deceived I was to engage in such a belief. As a child of God I have entered into His covenant. Would I not realize that He, as the greater party in the covenant, would supply for me what I needed?

God seems mysterious sometimes, but in His loving kindness He is able to impart to us the Gift of Faith (1 Corinthians 12:7-10) to help move impossible situations out of our lives. "Faith comes by hearing and hearing by the word of God" (Romans 10:17). As we begin to search and study God's word, we begin to hear God's promises and directions. Faith grows. We become encouraged, hope is birthed in our mind, and our way of thinking or perceiving is renewed (Ephesians 4:23). He gives us the faith and strength for every challenge.

As we stand in faith, fear will usually try to make an appearance. Fear likes to negatively move us into our future with *"What if..., I ought to..., or I should..."* It tries to paralyze and intimidate by manifesting as anxiety, panic, phobias, paranoia, delusions, agoraphobia, claustrophobia and more. Scripture tells us God is faithful (1 Corinthians 1:9); and as we choose to seek Him and learn to let go of the things that easily beset us, He promises to reward us (Hebrews 11:6). He truly desires to "give good things" to His children (Matthew 7:11).

It is also God's desire for us to have an intimate relationship with Him and to know Him (John 17:3). He is a righteous Father who forgives and heals us. When challenges surround me and

I feel alone, Psalm 103 encourages me and reminds me of our Father's wonderful nature and love. "Bless the Lord, O my soul; and all that is within me, bless His holy name...Forget not His benefits, Who pardons all your iniquities, Who heals all your diseases, Who redeems your life from the pit, Who crowns you with loving kindness and compassion; Who satisfies your years with good things, so that your youth is renewed like the eagle, He performs righteous deeds....He is compassionate and gracious, slow to anger and abounds in loving kindness...He has not dealt with us according to our sin...nor  rewarded us according to our iniquities...great is His loving kindness to those who fear Him..."

God once said to His prophet Isaiah that His people were in captivity for lack of knowledge (Isaiah 5:13). He also shared with Hosea that His people were destroyed for their lack of knowledge because they rejected knowledge (Hosea 4:6). God is telling us that we His people are often silenced or cut short by our lack of understanding, insight, or perception. So it is important for us to seek after truth and not dismiss revelation we receive. The wisdom and knowledge we need for life is found in His word, and as we choose to commit ourselves to the study and meditation of Scriptures, direction and answers to our questions and concerns will unfold.

Life is a journey of experiences with unexpected turns and twists. Sometimes we are able to make sense of what is presented to us and sometimes it is quite challenging and we enter into confusion and despair. Whatever life experiences we encounter, God wants us to have wisdom and understanding. He tells us to acquire knowledge. We are encouraged by God to search for Him and His truth; to ask Him for wisdom and to desire His revelation. His imparted knowledge will bring life, hope and vision to those who choose a quest to know Him. His words will build faith. The search for wisdom and truth can be long and arduous as well as frustrating; but when you find it, you will experience clarity, peace, comfort, and the Tree of Life.

## Negative Beliefs

Scripture may work for others but it won't work for me.

I don't really care what God says in His word. It isn't important for me.

God evidently doesn't care if I am well or not.

If He loves me so much and died for me, why do I hurt so much?

People expect me to be happy all the time.

I can never do enough for my family or God.

If I fail, I won't be loved.

If everybody else would just do what I want them to my life would be fine.

I can never live up to God's standards, so why try.

## Scriptural Truths

Understanding God's principles and precepts brings life.

My fear of rejection may keep me from embracing God's love and being able to sense the joy of His total acceptance.

When I am able to accept my weakness, God can then be strong in my life.

I will never find contentment trying to please others more than God.

## Scripture Meditations: "It is written..."

Proverbs 1:33 — "But he who listens to me shall live securely, and shall be at ease from the dread of evil."

Proverbs 4:20-23 — "My son, give attention to My words; incline your ear to My saying. Do not let them depart from your sight; keep them in the midst of your heart. For they are life to those who find them and health to all their body."

Proverbs 3:5-6 — "Trust in the Lord with all your heart, and do not lean on your own understanding. In all your ways acknowledge Him, and He will direct your path."

Isaiah 41:10 — "Do not fear, for I am with you; do not anxiously look about you, for I am your God. I will strengthen you, surely I will help you. Surely I will uphold you with My righteous right hand."

John 3:16 — "God so loved the world, that He gave His only begotten Son, that whoever believes in Him will not perish but have eternal life."

Luke 15:31 — "My child, you have always been with me, and all that is mine is yours."

## Reflections...

# 3
# DOES GOD REALLY WANT TO HEAL ME?

If you have endured pain or suffering, you have probably at one time or another entertained the question, *"Where are You, God, when I hurt?"* We often feel alone when we experience any kind of affliction or challenge, and during these times it is easy to consider jumping ship in our relationship with God. Fleeting thoughts pass through our minds as we think, *"Why did you let this happen?"* or *"If You are not going to help me then why should I believe in You?"* Discouragement and confusion try to assault our minds continually until we are able to resolve this issue in our heart concerning what we really believe about God, His character, and His healing nature. Studying and meditating on Scripture is always helpful, particularly when we become disillusioned or confused. Scripture holds the keys to our questions. So let's examine together some Scriptures as we begin to search to resolve questions we may have within our own hearts.

God is a loving Father who tells us over and over that He has great love and mercy toward His children. He is the Healer and He wants to see us walk in health. In 3 John 1:2 we are encouraged to prosper and be in health, even as our soul prospers. The multitudes followed Jesus everywhere, and Matthew 12:15 tells us Jesus "healed them all." We find throughout scripture encouragement God is the same, "yesterday, today and forever" (Hebrews 13:8). He never changes! He is still the Healer as stated in Exodus 15:26: "I, the Lord, am your Healer." God lovingly reminds us He is our health and our strength. His name, Jehovah-Rapha, forever proclaims He is the Lord of our health.

The Cross is our promise as Believers that the stripes Christ bore and the pain He suffered were for our health and healing. The crown of thorns pressed into his head and the blood that

poured down His forehead represent the pain in our mind and
emotions Christ bore for us so we can be free. Scripture states in
Isaiah 53:5: "He was pierced through for our transgressions, He
was crushed for our iniquities, the chastening of our well-being fell
upon Him, and by His scourging (stripes) we are healed."

## Questions Concerning Healing

*"But why isn't everyone healed?"* This is certainly the question of
the ages. Situations where we or loved ones have not been healed
have brought not only pain, but on occasion, condemnation and
pointing fingers. It has also brought thoughts of being rejected by
God:

> *"He does not love me."*
> *"He wants to punish me."*
> *"He has left me."*
> *"He is angry with me."*
> *"He doesn't keep His word."*
> *"I am not good enough to be healed."*
> *"What did I do wrong?"*
> *"I don't have enough faith."*
> *"I haven't worked hard enough for Him."*
> *"I haven't made Him happy."*
> *"He doesn't like me."*

The list of thoughts is endless. It is no wonder we doubt our
Father's love, feel rejected and walk away from His presence when
we entertain these beliefs. In the permanence of my own pain, I
walked away from God thinking He was not there anymore and He
didn't care. It was so difficult for me to believe and trust He really
meant that "He would never leave me or forsake me" (Deuteronomy
31:6). I felt so alone. *"Did He really love me? Did He really care?"*

God does not discipline us through sickness or disease.
Healing is the bread of God's children. God shares with us that He

is touched by the feeling of our infirmities (Hebrews 4:15). God is not happy we are in pain. We are reminded in Isaiah 53 that He bore our grief and sorrow and Christ took our iniquity on Himself, so with His stripes we are healed. God is good and He desires life for us because He loves us. Just as salvation is for everyone, healing is also available for everyone. If God wanted us to suffer and be sick, then why would James state in chapter 5:13-15: "Is anyone among you suffering? Let him pray. Is anyone cheerful? Let him sing praises. Is anyone among you sick? Let him call for the elders of the church and let them pray over him, anointing him with oil in the name of the Lord. And the prayer offered in faith will restore the one who is sick, and the Lord will raise him up, and if he has committed sins, they will be forgiven him."

When we examine David's life, we see the prophetic image of a man who made poor choices that brought heartache and pain to many; but in that pain, he became knowledgeable of the mercy and love of God as told in Psalm 103. He sang of the blessings and mercy of God who pardons all of our iniquities or sin, and who heals all of our diseases. David had a relationship with a loving God who redeemed his life from the pit and crowned him with His loving kindness and compassion. We must always remember - God never changes. He is the same, yesterday, today and forever. The love and grace He extended to David, is the same love and grace He extends to us today. God desires for us to know and experience His great love and faithfulness just like David.

It appears we sometimes forget the same Spirit that raised Jesus from the dead dwells in us according to Romans 8:11: "But if the Spirit of Him who raised Jesus from the dead dwells in you, He who raised Christ from the dead will also give life to your mortal bodies through His Spirit who dwells in you." How amazing! The very same Spirit of God, Holy Spirit, resides within all who acknowledge Him. As we meditate upon this Scripture, may we all receive a greater understanding of this truth as we allow it to become a living word in our lives.

There were seasons when it seemed I had a hook in my mouth

and no matter which way I turned, it hurt. During these times I found it difficult to embrace that God was a God of love. My perceptions of men and people in authority throughout my life left me with a sense that I had to earn their love, and if I was good enough or worked hard enough they would accept me. I often felt "used." Other times, I thought I had committed some unpardonable sin and that God was punishing me through my pain, sickness and loss.

When I gave my life to God, I unknowingly transferred my belief system to Him. I began to work for His approval and perform in various positions in the church to hopefully, someday, be good enough that He would finally bless me. With this mindset, within a few years I began to experience burnout with God. I developed performance anxiety because I didn't believe God was answering my prayers for healing; and if He wasn't answering them, it had to be because I was not behaving well enough to make Him happy.

Looking back, it is now clear how unbiblical my beliefs were about God my Father. What I believed was not the truth. It was my perception of events and experiences in my life. My responses and reactions to events formed my beliefs about myself and the world. Many of my beliefs were based on fear and pride. They were formed from the world's structures in what I observed, what I read and what I was taught. The world will try to tell us who we need to be, what we need to look like, and how we need to respond, but the real truth is in the Scriptures. It has taken time to meditate and study on these precious teachings, but they have helped me to understand the character of God and who I really am. Scripture tells us people perish for lack of knowledge. It is not God's desire for any to perish, but for all to experience His life. I would encourage you to meditate on the verses at the end of each chapter and ask Holy Spirit to renew your mind with God's truth and His desire for your life.

---

*"Father, I want to thank You for Your precious unconditional love. Thank You for Your word that teaches me about You. Please*

*forgive me for thinking You did not love me or want to heal me. I want to know You and understand Your ways. I surrender myself to You and ask You to renew my mind and heal the unhealthy ways I perceive life."*

## Negative Beliefs

I don't have enough faith for God to heal me.
I must do something good for God to love me.
I have sinned and God could never love me.
I must be special for God to love and heal me.
I did something wrong and God is punishing me.
God doesn't care about me.
I am alone in this world.
I must make it on my own.

## Scriptural Truths

God's provision is always perfect. He is never caught unaware. He is never surprised.
Healing is intimate and personal.
God does want my body and soul to prosper and be in health.
It is not necessary to prove my existence or validate my importance.
I am loved and accepted by God.
I can miss truth when I am defensive or in denial.
It is important when faced with conflict to find what I am really striving for – that will lead me to truth.
What I focus on, I make room for.
The keys to life are found in God's word.
I am acceptable to God and I am forgiven.

## Scripture Meditations: "It is written..."

John 1:12 — I am an adopted child of God.

Romans 5:1 — I have been justified (made innocent or free) and have peace (nothing between us) with God through Christ.

Romans 8:1 — I am free from condemnation in Christ.

Romans 8:28-29 — I know that all things work together for good for those that love God. I am called according to His purpose. He conforms me into His image.

Romans 8:35 — I am never separated from God's love for me.

Romans 8:37 — I am a conqueror through Christ's love.

1 Corinthians 3:16 — I am a temple of God and His Spirit dwells in me.

1 Corinthians 12:27 — I am of Christ's body.

1 Corinthians 6:17 — I am joined to the Lord and one in Spirit with Him.

1 Corinthians 6:19 — My body is a temple of the Holy Spirit.

1 Corinthians 6:20 — I have been bought with a price and I am God's.

2 Corinthians 6:1 — I work together with God.

2 Corinthians 1:21 — I am secure and anointed in God.

2 Corinthians 5:17 — I am a new creature in Christ; old things

have passed away and all things are new.

Colossians 1:14 — I have been redeemed and my sins are forgiven.

Colossians 3:3 — I am hidden with Christ in God.

Colossians 2:10 — I am complete in God.

Colossians 1:13 — I have been delivered from darkness and transferred to His kingdom.

Ephesians 1:5 — I am God's adopted child.

Ephesians 2:6 — I am seated in heavenly places with Christ.

Ephesians 2:10 — I am God's workmanship and I am created in Christ for His benefit and purpose.

Ephesians 2:18 — I have access to God through the Holy Spirit.

Philippians 1:6 — I am confident that God will perfect and finish the work He has begun in me.

Philippians 4:13 — I can do all things through Christ who strengthens me.

Hebrews 4:16 — I am confident that I may receive grace and mercy from God in my time of need.

1 John 4:13 — I abide in God and He abides in me.

## Reflections...

# 4
# TRIALS AND TESTING

I t can be difficult for us to acknowledge testing and trials as an aspect of God's nature; but as seen in Scripture as well as in reality, it does appear God sometimes allows the enemy to interfere in our lives so in His deliverance, our faith and trust in Him are enlarged. Just like taking an exam in school, the results of our test give us an idea of how much we have learned and where we may need to apply ourselves in more study.

When we examine the Scriptures concerning healing, we find conditions were sometimes attached to God's ability to heal. Those needing healing were instructed to perform an act of faith, as stretching out their hands, walking, or bathing in the river. In Exodus 15:26, God stated to the Israelites His conditions for health and healing by declaring: "If you will give earnest heed to the voice of the Lord your God and do what is right in His sight, and give ear to His commandments, and keep all His statutes, I will put none of the diseases on you." Verse 26 of that chapter actually reveals that God proved them or tested them.

When we look and listen for God's voice, it is good to "think it not strange concerning the fiery trial which is to try you, as though some strange thing happened unto you" (1 Peter 4:12). And as saints, the next verse can certainly cause us to feel uncomfortable when we read..."But rejoice, inasmuch as ye are partakers of Christ's sufferings; that, when his glory shall be revealed, ye may be glad also with exceeding joy."

How often we are condemned by our brothers and sisters for the trials we walk through; and yet, God is telling us we become partakers of Christ's suffering, His glory will appear and we will rejoice.

Certainly not all challenges are allowed for testing and

discipline. There have been times in my life when I have opened doors to sickness or loss by my own actions and choices. Numerous times I have become angry or I have chosen not to forgive. There have been times I have judged or been critical of others. Scripture is very clear that we must forgive so God can forgive us and when we choose to judge without repentance, we have placed ourselves in a position for judgment.

The book of Job is often used by well meaning people to give condemnation or discouragement to someone who is battling illness. They are generally the ones who like to say *"I told you so."* Some interpretations of Job's life teach that God gave the boils to Job and basically made his life miserable. But in Job 2:1-7 Scripture reveals that satan was the one who struck Job with the painful boils all over his body. God was not the one who gave Job the boils or sickness. There are many different teachings and beliefs as to why satan was allowed to touch Job, but as Scripture attests, it was not God. God is the one who knew Job as His servant, and He healed, blessed and restored Job.

## The Measuring Stick

Testing and trials are like a measuring stick. They stretch us and can encourage our faith. When we encounter a challenge or something painful in our lives, our reaction is measurable. How did I respond when I was cut off in traffic? How did I react when I heard the falsehood being spoken about me? When the clerk overpaid me, what did I do? If we will choose to examine ourselves we will be able to see by our response how we are growing in God's character and precepts. Holy Spirit is always working within us to reveal areas that God would like to touch and change. Our emotions are like the gauges on our car dashboard. When a red light flashes, we know there is something going on under the hood that we need to check. Emotions are neither good nor bad; they are just reactions to situations that show us how we feel and what we believe. If we will be aware of our responses and emotions, we can begin to check ourselves for things in our heart God would like us to address and work with Him to change. That is the good thing about our challenges and our responses. Whatever choices we have made or however we have responded, we can always repent and give them to God; and He will begin to redeem them by changing us inside in a remarkable way while helping us to mature in His love.

## Bad Things Can Happen to Good People

Sometimes there are horrific things that happen to good people and to children on this earth. There are not any easy answers when we experience challenges and conflict in our lives. Scripture tells us that God's ways are higher than our ways, so we will not always understand Him or the things He seems to allow.

I used to get very angry at God asking Him why He let particular things happen. As previously shared, I often looked at Him as a God of punishment and vengeance. I didn't have a relationship with Him or have a clue about His ways, I only saw and felt the hurt and pain. I became an observer of God, and I had minimal revelation that He was trying to communicate with me. It was life changing when I began to understand that God is very relational. He desires for us to know Him intimately and to go to Him about our concerns. He is not just a big mean bully watching and waiting for us all to make a mistake so He can delight in punishing us. He is love! Please hear these precious words spoken in 1 John 4:8 that declare to you that "God is love." He loves you! You are His beloved. The very essence of God and His nature is love. He loves His creation, and every action He makes is always performed in His beautiful and merciful love.

He has given those He created freedom and choices. Since Adam and Eve chose in the garden to rely on their own desires and intellect, the door was opened for evil to walk the earth. The universe is full of principles, equations and physics – laws that God has set up that He will not break. When those in society choose evil, they may experience pain by their own poor choices. God does not rejoice in anyone's pain or the consequences of unfortunate decisions. He suffers and weeps with us.

In every situation, God gives Himself the opportunity to reveal His love, kindness, mercy, goodness, provision, and all that He is. Looking back on trials I have encountered, I can now see how they have been used to change me and to give me the opportunity to grow and to mature in my relationship with Him. They have been used to strengthen my trust in Him and teach me more about His nature and character.

## Negative Beliefs

God would never test or challenge me.
What did I do to deserve this?
God just doesn't want me to be happy.
I haven't done anything wrong.

## Scriptural Truths

Sometimes I make choices that cause me to reap what I sow. I break God's spiritual and universal laws in my lack of understanding of God's principles.
God is a loving Father who desires for me to prosper and be in health.
Life will never be easy or without challenges.
I do not have to try to control everything to be at peace.
Life is not a product to attain things, but a journey to live and enjoy.
God is more interested in my character than in my gifting.

## Scripture Meditations: "It is written..."

James 1:2-4 — "Consider it all joy, brethren, when you encounter various trials, knowing that the testing of your faith produces endurance. And let endurance have its perfect result, that you may be perfect and complete, lacking in nothing."

Romans 15:13 — "Now may the God of hope fill you with all joy and peace in believing that you may abound in hope by the power of the Holy Spirit."

Psalm 9:9-10 — "The Lord also will be a stronghold for the oppressed, a stronghold in times of trouble, and those who know His name will put their trust in Him; For You, O Lord, have not forsaken those who seek You."

## Reflections...

# 5
# TIMING AND SEASONS

Timing and seasons are important to God as seen in the beautiful seasons of nature. As seasons come and go, they leave the earth changed as they bring the rain, cold, snow and warmth; leaving their signature as they continually change the contour of the land. We, like the earth, experience spring and summer seasons where life is full of hope, joy and anticipation of new things; as well as fall and winter, where things may begin to change or transition and we experience pain, loss, or hopelessness. Whatever season we are in, we also learn that they do not last forever as we learn to recognize and move with the ebb and flow of life. Jesus passed by the man who had been blind since birth. The disciples asked Him if this man's blindness had been caused by his parents' sin. The Lord answered not only had none of this man's family sinned, but that God had allowed the blindness in this man, so that God could be glorified (John 9:1-3). God desires to use every season in our life to mature us and to bring glory to Himself.

Ecclesiastes 3:1 tells us that "to everything there is a season." There is an appointed time for every event under heaven. Now this is not to say that if we are in a difficult situation we should choose or resolve to remain there. We are encouraged to always hope and look for God to bring life to us out of ashes. But how that may come, in what form it may come or what it may look like is what is often unsettling. When we are alone or afflicted, we often feel very isolated. How we respond to the isolation is part of our journey and part of our maturing in Christ.

By 1990, I found myself in a very difficult season of great physical and emotional pain. My first inclination was to fight. That is what I had been taught. But no matter how I tried to endure and resolve the pain, through medications, therapy, exercising, prayer, repentance or deliverance nothing seemed to give any relief. I became more anxious and fearful that I was never going to get any better. My mind began to tell me that I would be like this for the rest of my life. Panic and anxiety continued to rise up within me, *"Oh God, where are You? Why have You allowed this? What am I doing wrong? Do You hate me? Why are You punishing me?"*

## Embrace the Pain

Of course there were no answers. Using His excellent teaching skills, the Lord was quiet, gently encouraging me toward the path of revelation. I continued day in and day out in pain and by 1998 I began to sense my fighting and striving was waning. I found it difficult to hold on to hope. Was I giving up? Shouldn't I keep battling for this healing? Finally, in one short conversation, my dear younger brother encouraged me to *"embrace the pain."* At first this was an affront to my intellect and resolve. *"What? Embrace the pain?"* I exclaimed. *"Who in their right mind would ever do that?"* As I took a deep breath and repeated the thought, a peace came over me. *"Yes. Embrace the pain."* How simple. I had been battling something totally out of my control. I had tried performing for God, begging Him, coercing Him, trying everything in my mind to manipulate Him into healing me and removing the pain. My mind began to move out of fear into life. I began to breathe. I sensed my muscles beginning to relax. My anxiety lessened. I began to trust He knew what He was doing and He would reveal the truth in my distress. I began to rest. How strange it felt to choose to rest and begin to trust God was aware of me and my situation; and He would in His way, use everything for His good.

In this scary season of pain, God again revealed a part of Himself to me. He was my Father who loved me and He was using this situation to teach me to depend on Him. He showed me it was not necessary for me to perform for Him or cajole Him into doing my bidding; but He was very capable of making choices for me and teaching me His ways. He began to teach me the sense of resting in His arms, even in the midst of trials, knowing He was my provision, my health, my peace and supplier and He was ever present with me.

During the next ten years God continued His work in me and revealed many unhealthy and unscriptural beliefs. He showed me my fear of sickness and death. I began to see there were parts of my heart that were not yet sanctified and He in His loving and instructive way, was exposing in me those areas of unbelief and my lack of trust in Him. He also revealed my rebellion when I rejected and turned my heart away from His truths. I began to see that striving and relying on my own efforts for success needed to be given to Him for crucifixion. It had been exposed. My trust and my hope was really not in God, it was still in me.

Sin, which is nothing more than "missing the mark," may make us susceptible to sickness, but being sick or being in fiery trials does not always mean we are in sin. Let us all be cautious in making judgments, criticizing or pointing the finger at one another when only God knows how He is working in the hearts of all men. He may be correcting, but He may also be graciously teaching or instructing, sanctifying or purifying as He deals with each person. He allows situations of training to arise where He may reveal His character to us. It is certainly not our place to ever judge the work or timing of the Lord in any person's life.

## Seasons Perform a Special Work

Every child of God has seasons in their life in which God is doing a special work. Some seasons seem longer than others or more challenging than others. It is important to understand that the trial you may be going through will pass. As you walk through your trial you will be given a greater revelation of your Father's nature and character. He will reveal Himself to you as the Great Shepherd. He will teach you about His love and deliverance as well as His redemption. Look for Him. He will be very close to you and will change you. May we choose to encourage, support and pray for one another as we are transformed and matured by the ebb and flow of His Spirit.

During my personal trials and seasons, I have found it comforting to meditate on who God is by reading His names. Each day I would get up and say: *"I choose to trust You to take care of me today, especially during stress and trials."* Knowing His names, which reveal His nature and character, has brought me great hope and comfort, as well as praying this prayer:

> *"Father, forgive me for my lack of understanding and knowledge of Your ways. Help me to trust You and to understand Your nature and character, Your desires and Your plans. I want to know who You really are."*

## Negative Beliefs

I must do something good to get God to act on my behalf.

If I am not perfect for God, He will not be able to reward me.

I want to be in control because I can not trust God to look out for me.

God will punish me if I make a mistake.

## Scriptural Truths

God is merciful. His mercies are new every morning.

God will allow me to experience trials which help me develop my trust in Him.

Rebellion is like witchcraft in God's eyes. It can bring devastation to those who wield it or submit to it.

I am not controlled by my circumstances. I always have a choice in how I will respond and what I will choose to believe.

Facing my fears brings truth and allows me to choose freedom when I deal with fear.

Learning to give thanks in everything brings comfort and encouragement which gives life to my soul.

## Scripture Meditations: "It is written..."

Hebrews 12:5-11 — "Have you forgotten the exhortation which is addressed to you as sons, 'My son, do not regard lightly the discipline of the Lord, nor faint when you are reproved by Him; for those whom the Lord loves He disciplines, and He scourges every son whom He receives.' It is for discipline that you endure; God deals with you as with sons; for what son is there whom his father does not discipline? But if you are without discipline, of which all have become partakers, then you are illegitimate children and not sons. Furthermore, we had earthly fathers to discipline us, and we respected them; shall we not much rather be subject to the Father of spirits, and live? For they disciplined us for a short time as seemed best to them, but He disciplines us for our good, that we may share His holiness. All discipline for the moment seems not to be joyful, but sorrowful; yet to those who have been trained by it, afterwards it yields the peaceful fruit of righteousness."[2]

1 Samuel 15:22b-23 — "Behold, to obey is better than sacrifice, and to heed than the fat of rams. For rebellion as the sin of witchcraft and insubordination is as iniquity and idolatry."

## I Thank You God That In My Life You Are:

Jehovah-Adonai — "God - My Master and Lord" (Malachi 3:6)

Jehovah-El-Shaddai — "God - Who is more than enough" (1 Chronicles 29:11)

Jehovah-Jireh — "God - My Provider" (Genesis 22:14)

Jehovah-MaKaddish — "God - My Sanctifier" (Exodus 31:13)

Jehovah-Nissi — "God - My Banner of Love" (Exodus 17:15)

Jehovah-Rohi — "God - My Shepherd" (Psalm 23:1)

Jehovah-Rapha — "God - My Healer" (Exodus 15:26)

Jehovah-Shalom — "God - My Peace" (Hebrews 13:20)

Jehovah-Shammah — "God - Who is Present" (Ezekiel 48:35)

Jehovah-Tisidkenu — "God - My Righteousness" (Psalm 97:2)

## Reflections...

_____

_____

_____

_____

_____

_____

_____

_____

_____

_____

# 6
# PAIN AND SUFFERING

Pain, physical or emotional is never pleasant. I have heard many great men of God state they are not afraid of dying, but they do not look forward to the pain that may come as they age. Unanswered questions continue to abound concerning pain and suffering, particularly in the hearts of God's children. *"Have I done something wrong? Am I being punished? If You were really God You could stop this agony, so why don't You?"* As stated earlier, I do not personally have the answers to these age old questions. Scriptures do share that our walk with God may include suffering as well as loss. In my immaturity and lack of intimacy with God, I once believed He was out to get me and enjoyed extending my punishment. Years later, I have now resolved within my heart that God does not inflict pain upon us to get us to change or to punish us. He doesn't cause catastrophes and accidents to maim us or harm us. We often make poor or uninformed choices, disregarding His plan and His word, and pain can be the result. We sometimes ignore His universal laws that have a cause and effect. God is a redeemer and with His love, He desires to use situations for good and for redemption. Often pain is a motivating factor for us to seek wisdom and truth. God may use pain or the poor results of our actions to get our attention and cause us to consider change. He works on our character in our process of being transformed. His heart is always to redeem the earth. He says, "It is too small a thing that You should be My servant to raise up the tribes of Jacob, and to restore the preserved ones of Israel; I will also make You a light of the nations so that My salvation may reach to the end of the earth" (Isaiah 49:6).

When we experience pain, we are presented with choices to both search for truth and consider change, or to live in denial, blame and anger by pointing the finger at God or others. If we surrender ourselves to anger and blame, we align ourselves with satan's tactics of accusations and condemnation. When we choose to receive God's love, we align ourselves with forgiveness, redemption and restoration. His desire as a loving Father is for us to come to Him with our challenges and wounds and share our pain with Him. He is always near waiting for us to choose to sit with Him, share our woes and even cry on His strong shoulders. As we grow in our desire to understand and have relationship with God, He teaches us about His covenant and His exchange process called transformation. We give ourselves totally to Him and He fills us with His nature, character, and life. In other words He gives us all of Him. What a deal! When we truly give ourselves to God, we have signed up to experience all that He is, including the Cross: "that I may know Him, and the power of His resurrection and the fellowship of His sufferings, being conformed to His death" (Philippians 3:10).

## God's Covenant Exchange

I don't think anyone wants to suffer. Suffering has been a part of Scripture I always hoped to avoid. I didn't like it when people would read Scriptures about suffering with Christ. In fact, it took me many years to acknowledge that it was going to be a part of my Christian walk. Somehow, I had developed the belief that everything was going to be perfect once Christ came into my life. That if I asked and believed enough, all good things would flow my way. Sometimes God was more like a Santa Claus to me than a Savior. I was just sure if I was good, He was going to bring me all the gifts I desired. I now realize that a major part of my motivation for accepting Christ was less than lovely. I thought everything in my life was going to be happy, wonderful and perfect. I loved the warm feeling I had in His presence. I just wanted Him to take care of me and give me an easy life, but I did not realize He was going to want to change me. I was naïve in my covenant understanding to think He was going to do all of this for me and all I had to do was accept Him. In God's covenant exchange process, He gives us all that He is, but He now is able to take all of us. He begins a process of forming us into His image.

God never said our lives were going to be easy, but He did say He would always be there with us; and He would guide, comfort, deliver, heal, and restore us. He takes care of our needs – not always our wants. Looking back I can now see His presence and love was with me desiring to guide me to safety and healing, even in very painful and challenging situations.

## Jesus, Help Me!

Sometimes we are so overwhelmed with our problems or illness that we are almost incapacitated to cry out to God. I know there were days of pain, hopelessness, sickness and depression when I could only cry out *"Jesus, help me!"* He heard my plea and was there, picking me up and carrying me forward; giving me strength and hope to continue my search for His touch and truth.

There were other times of weariness when the pain almost became a security or a badge of honor for me to wear. Scripture told me God chastened the ones He loved, so I would learn to live in this pain and be an example for Jesus. It is important to check ourselves to be sure we have not submitted to a spirit of martyrdom or self-pity. If we think we must suffer for God to have Him love us, or believe as a Christian our life is supposed to be one of continual suffering, then we have not received the full revelation of the Cross and what Jesus accomplished for us.

No one will go through life without some challenges, trials or pain. The good news is that God is with us in those times of pain. He is the answer to them. I have met precious people who have been taught that a life of suffering somehow makes them more holy. God can certainly use hardships or illness to get our attention or to change our character, but it is not His will for us to endure a life of tragedy and loss to serve Him. He is a Father who wants to bless, heal, deliver, reveal, expose, restore and bring His resurrection life as He teaches and matures us into Christ's image.

Over the years I have observed that my challenges and times of darkness have brought me closer to God. When I'm well I often feel invincible; but when I am vulnerable, in my despair or woundedness, I have needed to look for the Master to help me, strengthen me and show me the way to His truth and life.

Jesus was moved with compassion to heal and deliver those who were demonized or oppressed; those who were unable to respond in faith, action or acknowledgement of His presence. Jesus' mercy and His grace oversaw and touched the very ones who were unable to respond in great faith. He still healed them. God is a lover of His creation and His desire is always to see us whole.

## Negative Beliefs

If I accept Christ, He will always take care of me and I will not experience any more trouble or pain.
As a Christian, I am supposed to have a care free life.
God will give me everything I want.

## Scriptural Truths

God gives me what I need, but not always what I want.
Life will have challenges and trials, but God will never leave me or forsake me. He is always walking with me through each moment.
God's love brings peace and joy.
There is usually some truth in every situation if I will look for it.
God's love does not have conditions. He loves me unconditionally.
It is spiritually arrogant to condemn myself, when in doing so, I really am denying the sacrifice at the Cross by Christ.

## Scripture Meditations: "It is written..."

Romans 8:14-15 — "For all who are being led by the Spirit of God, these are sons of God. For you have not received a spirit of slavery leading to fear again, but you have received a spirit of adoption as sons by which we cry out, 'Abba, Father!'"

1 Peter 4:12 — "Friends, when life gets really difficult, don't jump to the conclusion that God isn't on the job. Instead, be glad that you are in the very thick of what Christ experienced. This is a spiritual refining process, with glory just around the corner." (Message Bible)

1 Corinthians 1:9 — "God is faithful, through whom you were called into fellowship with His Son, Jesus Christ our Lord."

Deuteronomy 31:8 — "And the Lord is the one who goes ahead of you. He will be with you. He will not fail you or forsake you; do not fear or be dismayed."

Philippians 1:6 — "For I am confident of this very thing, that He who began a good work in you will perfect it until the day of Christ Jesus."

Romans 8:35-39 — "Who shall separate us from the love of Christ? Shall tribulation, or distress, or persecution, or famine, or nakedness, or peril or sword? Just as it is written, 'For Thy sake we are being put to death all day long; we were considered as sheep to be slaughtered.' But in all these things we overwhelmingly conquer through Him who loved us. For I am convinced that neither death, nor life, nor angels, nor principalities, nor things present, nor things to come, nor powers, nor height, nor depth, nor any other created thing, shall be able to separate us from the love of God, which is in Christ Jesus our Lord."

1 Peter 2:24 — "And He Himself bore our sins in His body on the cross, that we might die to sin and live to righteousness; for by His wounds you were healed."

## Reflections...

_____

_____

_____

_____

_____

_____

_____

_____

_____

_____

_____

_____

_____

_____

_____

_____

_____

_____

_____

# 7
# FAITH AND RELATIONSHIP

We all have experienced family, friends, children and people of great faith who have by the world's standards lost their battle with severe illness. Where was God during these horrible times? How could God let this happen? We battle these questions at some point in life, and after much contemplation we usually end up acknowledging we still don't really have an answer. God seems very far away and mysterious to us. We have learned to focus on building our faith or memorizing Scriptures more than developing our relationship with Him. Throughout Scripture we see God reaching out to us with His desire for relationship, but we often are more concerned with our religious doctrines and teachings than learning about who He is.

We all inhabit a body of flesh and we all will come to a point of death in this life. It is part of our process and journey toward our heavenly home that defines us as being God's children. God does not always reveal His plan in our battles against sickness. But one of our battles is that of faith; to believe God as our Father has a great plan that reaches out to touch not only ourselves but all of humanity and eternity.

Paul, in 2 Timothy 4:7 declares: "I have fought the good fight, I have finished the course, I have kept the faith." How, when we are in these trials, do we keep our faith? Trials come to steal, kill and destroy us, but in Hebrews 12:2 we are encouraged that Jesus is the "author and perfecter of our faith." I have come to realize God is really our faith. His name is Faith. He tells us all we need is the faith of a mustard seed to please Him. How small is that? It is a little larger than the period at the end of this sentence.

# Faith and Lack of Confidence

In Matthew 17:14-22, when the disciples tried to heal the demoniac and were rebuked by Jesus, He was not rebuking them for their faith. The Greek translation of the word faith or "littleness of your faith" in Matthew 17:20 means lack of confidence.[3] They lacked confidence in their skills. Jesus shared all they needed was mustard seed faith and nothing would be impossible. I personally believe His true rebuke to them was not only for their lack of confidence, but also their lack of discernment, when He states in verse 21, "this kind does not go out except by prayer and fasting."

Can you see Jesus sitting there saying, *"Now guys, how long is it going to take for you to remember what I've taught you? We've been together awhile now and you have experienced many miracles and healings, and yet you still don't have any confidence. Remember you can't always just pray or rebuke the enemy for healing; sometimes you have to fast and pray. How long is it going to take you to get this? Where is your discernment? Have you been fasting or in prayer?"* Jesus was reminding them of the things He had taught them: to be confident in their gifts, to use discernment against the demonic forces, and to know when to fast and pray for healing and deliverance.

There are times when my trust and faith have wavered with doubt and unbelief. I have battled the fear of death as I believe many do. What is heaven really going to be like? Is death going to be painful? As God's children we are encouraged to view loss or death not as failure, but as the gateway to maturity and ultimately to our heavenly home. We are human. We are learning to lean on Him. When we receive Christ, we begin to step into God's spiritual realm and we begin a journey of the life in the Spirit appearing more real to us than life here on earth. That is our process of maturing and of becoming more like Christ. It is important for us to learn to trust Him; and it is comforting that even though we suffer pain, illness or loss of life or vision we are partakers of His victory. "O death, where is thy victory, O death where is thy sting? Death is swallowed up in victory" (1 Corinthians 15:54-55).

I have often spent too much time playing out past mistakes and events in my mind. *"If I would have only done this; if I had only had more faith. I should have tried this."* I never allowed myself to forget things in my life. It never occurred to me to forgive myself. I held onto wounds and pain like a badge of honor. And in the heat of an argument, I would either attack myself or make sure I reminded my husband of all the pain he put me through, so I could get in one more thrust of the knife. It is rare to be given a "do-over" in life or to be able to take back the things of our past. A lot of mental and emotional energy can be wasted blaming or talking about what could have been. Demonic activity loves to attach itself to our pain with torment and thoughts of regret. Meditating on things we cannot undo often leads to depression and anxiety. I allowed years of listening to regrets like: *"You should have..., Why didn't you..., If you would have only...,"* to confuse and exhaust me. Living with disappointment or with an unending list of things we should be doing or accomplishing leads to despair. God doesn't call Himself I WAS or I WILL BE. He calls Himself I AM. He does not live in the past, so for us to peacefully abide in His presence we must choose to give old decisions and memories to Him and learn to focus on the present. It is important for us to choose to believe the truth of His word and expose the lies we have believed as we choose to be free.

Jesus stands with us, posing the same question He asked His disciples: "How long before you understand what I have taught you? I love you and I am faithful. I have given the same measure of faith to all My children and all you need is the mustard seed that you have. Be confident in Me, learn to discern the spirits and together we will move mountains. You have all the faith and everything you need, because I live in you," (Matthew chapter 17).

God's word is filled with evidence of His will to heal us. From the lame, the broken-hearted, the leper, the blind, the deaf, and the demonized; God is willing and ready to touch all manner of sickness with His healing power. God is our Healer and though we may not always understand His ways or provision, He does want us to walk in health and wholeness.

## Religion Versus Relationship

Many of us have been taught God is up in heaven looking down at us just waiting for us to slip up. We fear He is ready at any minute to punish us for our mistakes or faults. That is the voice of error talking to your mind. God is a loving God who desires a relationship with you. He wants to talk with you, play with you, sense the earth through you, guide you, love you, teach you, and protect you.

Religion taught me God was way up in heaven. He was very busy with little time for me and He was waiting on me to have a problem so He could correct me and tell me *"I told you so."* Religion taught me it was important to God for me to try to be perfect so I could receive His love. I perceived that when I was busy and doing things for Him, He would love me more. Religion told me no matter how hard I tried I would never be acceptable to God and that when I failed He would walk away and leave me alone in the desert.

The Spirit taught me God is full of faith and He is ever present, always concerned about how I feel and what I am doing. He wants to talk with me and express Himself in my daily affairs. He wants to have an intimate loving relationship with me where I can share the longings of my heart as well as my pain; and He can share His love and desire for me through His guidance and gentle correction. He wants to guide us into the truth of who we really are. His desire is to have a relationship with you also. He is anxious and patiently waiting to work with you throughout your day, to help you solve your problems and guide you in your daily life as He reveals wisdom and revelation to you.

How do you begin to have a relationship with God? Acknowledge He is there with you. Begin to share with Him what you are feeling or what you are looking forward to. Ask Him things about Himself. What does He like? What does He see? How does

He feel? Tell Him what you think of Him. Let Him tell you what He thinks of you. Take time to listen. He will speak to you in nature, in the wind, through friends and animals. He will speak to you through Scriptures and through the prophetic word. He will visit you and speak to you through your dreams or visions you may see in your mind's eye. Write down the quiet thoughts in your mind as you listen and are still. Our Father's voice is gentle yet strong. He speaks with encouragement, love, hope and direction. He may come to you with correction or conviction, but He will never speak to you with anger or condemnation. He is peaceful and nurturing; He never forces or pushes us into decisions or actions. Be patient, wait and watch. He will reveal Himself. He loves to visit with those who visit Him.

*"Father, thank You that You love me, and that You are always faithful and merciful to me. I sometimes am afraid and I think I am alone. I begin to lack confidence in You and I become confused. I know I cannot accomplish anything alone and that I need You. I choose to trust You today Lord. I know you want me to succeed, to be healthy, and restored. I believe Father, please help my unbelief."*

## Negative Beliefs

God is out there somewhere in the sky too busy to care about me.
God must not care about sickness or people getting hurt with all the tragedies in the world.
God doesn't talk to people.
There is no such thing as demons.

## Scriptural Truths

God's desire is to have a relationship with me.

He has sent Holy Spirit to teach me, guide me, counsel me and
   speak to me.

When I choose evil actions, I may be experiencing demonic
   oppression.

When I break God's universal laws there are natural and spiritual
   consequences.

My faith and trust grows as God reveals Himself to me through
   my experiences with Him.

Conflict is sometimes necessary to help me see truth and resolve
   toxic thoughts.

God is not interested in my good works, but in my relationship
   with Him.

I can miss God's blessings when I do not understand His desire
   for relationship.

Sensing peace within me can help me to navigate through my
   decision making.

## Scripture Meditations: "It is written..."

Joel 2:25-26 — "Then I will make up to you for the years that the
   swarming locust has eaten, the creeping locust, the stripping
   locust, and the gnawing locust, My great army which I sent among
   you. And you shall have plenty to eat and be satisfied, and praise
   the name of the Lord your God who has dealt wondrously with
   you; Then My people will never be put to shame."

1 John 3:20 — "In whatever our heart condemns us; God is greater
   than our heart, and knows all things."

Psalm 46:1 — "God is our refuge and strength, a very present help
   in trouble."

Psalm 34:15 — "The eyes of the Lord are upon the righteous, and
   his ears are open unto their cry."

Isaiah 40:29-31 — "He gives strength to the weary, and to him who lacks might He increases power. Though youths grow weary and tired, and vigorous young men stumble badly, yet those who wait for the Lord will gain new strength; they will mount up with wings like eagles, they will run and not get tired, they will walk and not become weary."

2 Timothy 2:13 — "If we are faithless, He remains faithful; for He cannot deny Himself."

Hebrews 12:1-2 — "Therefore, since we have so great a cloud of witnesses surrounding us, let us also lay aside every encumbrance, and the sin which so easily entangles us, and let us run with endurance the race that is set before us, fixing our eyes on Jesus, the author and perfecter of faith, who for the joy set before Him, endured the cross, despising the shame, and has sat down at the right hand of the throne of God."

## Reflections...

# 8
# GOD'S DIVERSITY IN HEALING

It is important to understand God is very diverse as well as creative in His ability to heal. Throughout Scripture, Jesus healed in various ways including touching, speaking, declaring, decreeing, giving conditions of obedience or mandates and rebuking demonic activity. When He healed the Roman soldier's servant, Jesus did not even see or meet with the servant. The faith of the soldier and His understanding of Jesus as Lord and Healer touched Jesus' heart of compassion. As Jesus healed the servant from afar, He showed us healing has no distance and that His healing power came from God. He declared the servant healed and he was (Matthew 8:5-13). God's healing touch comes in many forms and is quite diverse, and most healings we experience are progressive. As I searched for my own healing, I began to experience some of the various ways God brings wholeness to His children.

## Seek and You Shall Find

When we accepted Christ, we began to walk in the spiritual world as well as our natural world. Being made of spirit, soul and body, we now must be open to search for truth in our spiritual life, our soul and emotional life as well as in our body. We are encouraged to "examine ourselves" (1 Corinthians 11:28) and to "ask and it shall be given unto you; seek and you shall find; knock, and it shall be opened to you" (Matthew 7:7). In our search for truth, let's begin to look at God's diversity of healing and the many ways He may come to us with His healing virtue.

We all have experienced healing sometime in our lives. In my personal journey I received various touches of healing from God and found our Father to be loving, merciful, gracious and kind.

He is Jehovah-Rapha – the Lord our Healer, and I believe He finds great joy and pleasure in touching us, redeeming us, and restoring us.

Healing does not always come by way of the miraculous, although I think most of us would like all our physical and emotional challenges to leave in an instant. Most healings are a process. Whether we are healed through diet changes, herbs, exercise, physical therapy, medicine, surgery, counseling, prayer, deliverance or a miracle; it is important to be open to the many diverse ways God may appear with His healing touch.

During a healing revival I was attending, I once heard a pastor say that God does not heal us to go back to do the same thing we were doing before. He heals us to serve Him and to become a vessel for His Kingdom to be manifested in the earth. It is important for us to understand God has a purpose for us. He doesn't heal us to return to our old ways or to our old habits. He heals us to be a marker for Him; to be a testimony of His glory, love and greatness here on earth.

## Modern Medicine - Science

I experienced one of my first touches of healing when I was five years old. I developed Rheumatic Fever from a strep infection. I remember being hospitalized and lying flat in my bed at home for many weeks. My parents were told I would need to be kept very still to discourage any damage to my heart. Weeks passed while I remained in bed. We lived next door to my elementary school and I remember lying there, peering out through the large window, watching my classmates play at recess. *Why did I get this terrible illness? Would my heart be damaged? Would I live through this? Where was God?* I'm sure my parents at times felt anxiety and concern. *What if they had not taken me to a doctor? What if the doctor did not have the knowledge to identify this illness and get me to a hospital?* Penicillin had just been discovered a few years before and was now prescribed for this disease. *What if it had not been discovered or developed through medical research and scientific studies?*

I am grateful to medicine and to physicians for being there for me when I am ill. Their diagnostics and treatment techniques are gifts from God. I am thankful for my dentist who can take care of my teeth and to my pharmacist who provides the proper medications when I need them. In Ezekiel, Isaiah, Matthew, Luke and Revelations, there is evidence that herbs and oils were used for medicinal purposes and there were people who administered these healing salves and ointments to save the sick.

God is not against medicine or doctors. If we believe He is the Creator of all things, then He created medicine and gives His knowledge and wisdom to our physicians. He has provided them as another avenue or door through which we may be healed. Physicians have been trained to be excellent diagnosticians. Technology and medical knowledge have developed at amazing speed to not only diagnose but to heal various diseases. Prayer has also been important to me in preparing for visits, examinations and procedures, asking God to work through the physician and give them wisdom and revelation concerning the situation.

One of God's names that He reveals to His people as stated earlier is Jehovah-Rapha (Jehovah My Healer). He may touch us with a miracle or He may supply the answers to our medical needs through other doors. He also is Jehovah-Jireh (Jehovah My Provider), for He supplies for us the means that we need to be healed. What a wonderful Father He is! God pours out His love and truth, and through His names declares and reveals His character, nature, and power to us. He is our Healer and the Provider of all our needs.

When we are battling sickness or disease we will be faced with examining our own trust and faith. There have been many times of reflection when I have observed my own lack of faith and trust. It was discouraging and there were times I felt ashamed that I could not be strong or trust God more. I was disappointed in my weakness and lack of resolve. God was not trying to shame me for a lack of faith. He knew exactly how I felt and He still loved me.

Our lives are a process of developing our faith in God by learning to trust Him through each adversity that we face. Sometimes it is difficult to have what we believe is "enough faith" for impossible situations to be removed from our lives. I have been told more times than I wish to remember that I did not have enough faith for God to act on my behalf and that was why I did not receive healing. This kind of thinking brought me face to face with rejection and judgment from my brothers and sisters in Christ and planted within my heart negative seeds that God did not love me, and He only cared about healing me if I was good. I know God honors our faith in Him and fortunately for our sake He asks only for the faith of a "mustard seed." God has given us all the same measure of faith. We all have enough faith to believe and trust Him. He is our Faith. And if we need more faith He is the one who imparts that extra measure of faith or the gift of faith for the miracles in our lives to take place.

In 1998 when I attended a healing meeting and needed a miracle in my body, I cannot say that I personally had enough faith to trust God to touch me. I sat there in the pew wishing God would be kind enough or merciful enough to help me. I wondered if I had been obedient enough or if God would pass me by. Through the years I have found it can be difficult to muster up enough faith when you have continually been assaulted by sickness or disease. So I sat there and told Him I didn't think I had enough faith to believe He would touch me. *"Father would you please help my unbelief."* Right there in the pew an energy and hope began to form within me. Through a word of knowledge (information God gives you concerning the past or present), the pastor called out my physical problem and I immediately found my legs carrying me up to the platform. God did for me what I could not do for myself. I began to realize then, God was love and He wanted to show me His mercy and grace.

In God's covenant with us, He, being the greater party, chooses to take care of us. We are the weaker party in this relationship and by His grace He provides for us what we cannot muster up or do for ourselves. There have been times of trials when I was too exhausted to pray or draw upon any faith or hope, but God in His mercy never leaves us or forsakes us. He is always there in our challenges and trials. We may not understand the circumstances we are in and the outcomes may not always be what we hoped, but God is faithful. If you are in need of strength or faith, ask Him for it. He says He will not withhold any good thing from those who believe in Him. As He continues His work in our lives we can give glory to Him and choose to trust Him.

I once was trying so feverishly to be healed of my chronic pain. I found myself constantly in a doctor's office or thinking of who I could go to next who might just have the answer for my relief. The need for healing began to consume me as I constantly read articles, tried diets, exercise, medications, prayer, physical therapy, and fasting...anything was open game. Anxiety and panic began to overtake me. I was discouraged and alone. I would cry out daily, *"God, where are you?"* Then, one day I heard the sweet quiet voice within my thoughts whisper – *"You're seeking the healing instead of the Healer."* Ouch, that hurt. What truth and revelation confronted me. I was so consumed in getting my healing I had totally lost sight of my Savior. "Seek first His Kingdom and His righteousness and all will be added unto you" (Matthew 6:33).

## Nutrition - Herbs

My father was diagnosed with lymphocytic leukemia in the early 1980's. Chemotherapy was not yet recommended for him, but the prognosis was of concern. I watched as my mother began researching avenues of healing for my father through medical and natural arenas. She soon came in contact with a nutritionist who also owned a health food store. After much prayer and counsel, they chose to investigate the alternatives for healing through a change of diet. My parents made the choice to cleanse their bodies and reform their way of eating through a specialized diet enriched with nutrients and enzymes. They traveled to meetings and attended training on proper diet and cooking methods and they sought nutritional advice on their specific dietary needs. They removed white sugar, white flour and rice, processed foods and lunch meats, carbonated drinks, milk products, fried food, saturated fats, margarine, alcohol, cheese, artificial sweeteners and red meat from their diets. They began to take vitamins to restore nutrients. Raw vegetables, fruits, whole grain breads, distilled water, brown rice and soy products were the staples of their special diet.

As months passed, trips to the doctor and blood reports became more positive. These circumstances caused us to examine our own lifestyles and eating habits. We became more conscious of reading food labels and checking the different chemical additives. I watched my mother and father change their eating habits and food intake. There were daily trips to the grocery for fresh vegetables and most meals were cooked at home. Fast food was a rare occasion. My father did not have to undergo chemotherapy or any other medical interventions for this disease and he lived a long and healthy life for over twenty years.

Not all illnesses will be totally healed from diet or exercise. However, in the book of Leviticus we find God has given keys to consider when choosing our food. These diet and sanitary laws still contain truths that can help guide us today in a lifestyle of healthy eating.

I know my parent's diet looks severe to some, and not everyone may believe that it is necessary to manage our diets at this level; but as 1 Corinthians 10:23 instructs: "Everything is permissible - but not everything is beneficial." God's dietary laws in Leviticus were not given to Israel for punishment, but for common sense to keep them healthy through the struggles and stress they would encounter. Some may say they are Old Testament instructions that do not apply to us because we are not under the old law. However, they are still God's words, and they were given to encourage us to use common sense and be actively responsible for what we put in our bodies.

We live in the "land of plenty" but that does not mean

everything is good for us. We are spirit beings, but we live in a real and natural world. Our bodies are exposed to toxins and chemicals which may attack and weaken our healthy bodies and immune systems. Our farm fields are continually used for food sources draining the nutrients from the ground. We can be a part of supporting our bodies in good health or undermining them with our poor eating habits. Shall we be wise and examine our habits to see if what we eat produces life or death in our natural bodies? There are many excellent doctors, nutritionist and books available today. If you ask, God will guide you into all truth and direct you toward the best diet and nutrition for your needs. It is good to gain insight and knowledge by reading and staying abreast of healthy lifestyle choices and eating.

I am the first to admit I love chocolate, and an ice cream cone on a warm day is so gratifying. A piece of apple pie a la mode, fried chicken or a slice of delicious cheesecake can certainly make my mouth water. However, any of these eaten in excess may do harm to my system. Everyone has read articles on the concerns with sugar, coffee and caffeine, too much red meat, eating no meat at all, chemicals in our water, toxic cleaning agents, and the poor air quality that we breathe. We certainly do not want to become extreme and close ourselves off in a bubble, but we can read, study, and listen to our bodies speaking to us. Seek out a good nutritionist and consider learning to eat and live wisely.

Throughout the Old Testament God shares about the many herbs He has given to man. In Romans 14:2 it states that "One man has faith that he may eat all things, but he who is weak eats vegetables only." After seeking a nutritionist for my own chronic pain, I learned the human body has a PH balance and mine was unstable. By eating a diet which was plentiful in certain fruits, vegetables and whole grains, taking nutritional supplements and ceasing my cola, sugar and white flour intake; I began to experience less stress and pain in my body, particularly my legs and joints.

My physician once noticed my B vitamin levels were low. He administered B12 shots for a short period of time and I continued with B complex supplements. I began to feel more emotional peace. Because my body was receiving better nourishment, I became more alert. I found I was thinking more clearly and I had more energy. I was also less susceptible to colds and I even lost some weight. Please be reminded that nutritional supplements as well as prescribed medicine may have side effects. They also may not always interact well with each other. As always, it is good to check with your physician, pharmacist or nutritionist for any possible harmful interactions or possible allergic reactions.

Much of the nutritional value in our food is lost during processing. The length of time that it takes to get the food to market and into our homes has dramatically changed from the days when the neighborhood market carried fresh fruits and vegetables. Continual farming of the land has left the soil depleted of natural nutrients and minerals that we need for our bodies to be healthy and strong. Even much of our live stock is injected with numerous hormones and antibiotics, while our produce is sprayed with pesticides. By the time we get our vegetables, fruits and grains from the market, many of the nutrients and enzymes have been lost. With this knowledge, it makes sense to investigate the need for eating healthy, nutritious food and consider taking nutritional supplements to help ensure our bodies are getting proper nutrition.

When our son was in third grade he became very ill. After numerous trips to the doctor and three rounds of antibiotics, he was not any better and was on the verge of developing pneumonia. He exhibited dark circles under his eyes, difficulty breathing, chronic cough and fatigue which alarmed us. What were we going to do? Nothing seemed to be "working."

After little change with the antibiotics we decided to take our son to our nutritionist.[4]  A saliva and urine test was taken. The results showed our son had pre-diabetic symptoms. It was concluded that a diet change was one of the courses of action. For one week, he was taken off sugars, soft drinks, white flour, fried foods, meats and dairy. His meals consisted of mainly fresh salads and distilled water. Little by little, we were able to add chicken, eggs, whole wheat bread and other grains. Eating nutritiously helped support and strengthen his immune system and within a few weeks he was healed and back to his normal activities.

My husband, Richard, loves tennis. He has played tennis, as well as taught lessons, for most of his life. I've observed athletes and sports enthusiasts who are used to periodic pain as they exercise, but one day the pain he experienced was excruciating. When he walked or tried to run, he would experience pain in the back of his heel. Reducing exercise or increasing his stretching program gave him only minimal relief. After being diagnosed with three heel spurs, he began researching different possible avenues for healing. He discovered research articles over the internet that discussed the importance of certain calcium supplements. He faithfully took his calcium supplements each day and months later, his heel spur pain left and he has not had any reoccurring pain.

Now all this is not said to guilt anyone into changing their diets or ingesting numerous supplements. Other individual's experiences, knowledge, insight, discussions and research can give us knowledge to help make quality decisions for ourselves and our family's health. God has told us that we as His people are destroyed for lack of knowledge (Hosea 4:6) and in James 1:5 we are encouraged to ask for wisdom in our lack. God gives His wisdom generously to all who ask. Taking the time to search out information and obtain counsel will help lay a solid foundation and prepare you for future decisions.

It is challenging today for families to choose to eat healthy and nutritious meals. It is so easy with our time restraints and schedules to just go out or pick up food that is already prepared. I enjoy dining out and I get sweet cravings that sometimes cry out for a chocolate milk shake or a tasty donut! I particularly crave these sweet treats in times of stress. When I am very busy or overwhelmed I have noticed my tendency to want to go back to my old eating habits. It has been a struggle to eat well. However, as my diet has improved and I have become more aware of my eating habits, it has become easier to maintain a healthy weight. My muscle spasms, joint pain, headaches, sinus drainage, foggy brain, fatigue and other ailments have also diminished over the years. We have available today a wealth of knowledge to help us make healthier choices, as we become more conscious of the need to take care of our bodies and minds through proper diet and nutrition.

There has always been great debate concerning the dietary laws of the Old Testament verses the freedom of the New Testament covenant. Some people believe using Old Testament Scripture puts one under the law, bringing bondage and legalism. However, Jesus states in Matthew 5:17: "Do not think that I came to abolish the law and the prophets, I did not come to abolish, but to fulfill the law." The word "fulfill" (Pieroo-Greek) means to fully enforce and explain it. Jesus came not only to fulfill prophecy but He also came to perform or demonstrate the law, to explain it and enforce it.

It is not my purpose to persuade or dissuade anyone on this issue or to debate Scripture. I do believe God has given us a great deal of information regarding our diet through Scriptures and through science and medicine. There is wisdom and knowledge available to study and apply in our daily lives. Gaining understanding will assist us as we search for wisdom and truth concerning healing and health for our body, soul, and our spirit.

## Exercise - Stretching

Almost any day in a magazine or newspaper, one can read of the benefits of exercise. Exercise is as important to our bodies as proper eating. We were made to work and have physical activity daily. During the years I suffered great pain and muscle spasms, it was not an easy task to exercise; almost every movement brought pain. It was discouraging. I would often want to give up. After a person receives surgery in a hospital, what is one of the first things they do to the patient? The nurse comes in within hours of the procedure and gets the patient up and moving; because medical science knows it is important to get the body and all its systems stimulated and functioning for optimum healing.

There were seasons in my life where I suffered so much pain I would lie in bed afraid to move. The muscle spasms were excruciating and I was tired of the pain and suffering. I thought if I could just lie there long enough or still enough, maybe the pain would finally go away and I would be able to rest. In choosing to be immobile I prolonged my suffering, because my body quickly began to atrophy. I began to lose muscle mass. As my body weakened so did my mental state. I became very depressed and anxious about my health and pain. I knew I had to make a decision to begin getting out of bed and to begin moving no matter how great the pain. Little by little, I regained some of my strength. Combining stretching with my exercise and aerobic routines helped my flexibility and agility as well as my mind. Exercising began to feed needed oxygen to my body and stimulate various chemicals which elevated my mood. I began to feel encouraged and some of my depression began to lift. I found out exercise is not only good for our muscles and organ functions, but it releases endorphins in our body. These chemicals activate and stimulate our neurotransmitters in the pleasure center of our brain which actually lift our mood and emotions. Even perspiration from exercise helps rid our bodies of toxins that build up within our system. Our bodies are beautifully and wonderfully made. Every part of us is made to work together as a beautiful symphony giving life. God has placed within our bodies the means for them to heal. Finding the diet and exercise plan is a personal journey and a personal decision. From proper diet, exercise and nutritional supplements, we can assist our bodies in the healing process. Always be sure to seek out medical and professional help before you begin making any changes in your lifestyle. If you search and ask for wisdom and truth, you will find it.

## The Lump - Gift of Healing and Miracles

There are many doors to healing, and it is important to always be encouraged to search through them all. We never really know how God will choose to touch a person. There is no one formula that brings healing or a miracle. As we have discussed, some may come through medical science, nutrition, a healthy diet and exercise. Others may simply occur as the body naturally heals itself. Some healings may also come through the Gift of Healing or Gift of Miracles (1 Corinthians 12:9-10).

I was experiencing a very painful lump in my breast which had appeared in what seemed to be overnight. I trusted it would go away and it would be nothing to worry about. Months passed, and the fear inside my thoughts of what this lump might represent began to grow. It became very inflamed to the point that even a bed sheet at night would be painful. I do not recommend this type of response to anyone. It would have been wise for me to seek medical attention and diagnosis. But just like times before, instead of facing my fear or pain, I chose to ignore it in hopes that it would go away. My anxiety began to rise and I knew I was going to have to see a physician soon. My local church was having a healing revival with Pastor Billy Burke.[5] I felt encouraged to attend. The first night there were many miraculous healings. One small boy's eyesight was fully restored. Another gentleman was freed from a respirator and oxygen tank. Many received freedom from pain and arthritis in their bodies. All of a sudden, he called out a word of knowledge that someone was experiencing pain in their breast. As stated earlier, a word of knowledge is information God gives you concerning the past or present. I sat there stunned. I couldn't move. Fear, embarrassment, and unbelief swept through me. I couldn't go up there and let anyone know what I was dealing with. Another lady quickly went forward and received healing from painful cysts in her breast. *Why wasn't that for me? Why didn't I go up?*

After the meeting I drove home angry at myself that I had not trusted enough to see if God would touch me. I made a decision in the car that I would go back the next night. If he would call out my circumstance I would go forward.

It was July 21, 1998 and as I entered the church I felt an

excitement in me but also a fear. *What if he didn't call out my problem? What if he did? Would I go forward? Would I be afraid? Would I be embarrassed? Would I have enough faith?* The pastor gave his message. It was a message about unbelief. How wonderful to hear that others sometimes had difficulty with their faith too. As he finished, he asked us all to pray with him. The only thing I remember was the end of the prayer – *"Father, help my unbelief."* I felt relieved that I could actually tell God I might not have enough faith to trust Him. It was like the secret was out and I didn't have to hide anymore. There it was. *"God, I want to trust You, but I don't know if I can. I want to be healed, but I don't know if You will. Help me God. Help my unbelief!"*

The meeting continued as many afflicted individuals were touched with healing. Eye sight was restored. Back pain vanished. People were jumping up and down in their relief and excitement that they had been healed. It was beautiful to watch. I was encouraged in the goodness of God and began to see that miracles really do take place.

Suddenly, the pastor said, *"There is someone here with a lump in their breast."* Adrenaline pulsed through my body. I jumped out of the pew and ran to the platform. It was like an out of body experience watching myself react to his declaration as I ran down the aisle. The next thing I remember was someone picking me up off the floor. It seemed like I had run into an invisible force that knocked me to the ground. I had blanked out, like a quick slumber that lasted a nanosecond. *"Pick her up"* he commanded. I remember two men trying to help me up as I staggered to my feet. All of a sudden I was moving in slow motion. I was trying to focus on the pastor who was talking to me. My mind was foggy and I could not see him clearly. I sensed an invisible weight upon me like I was being awakened from a deep sleep. *"Check your lump please,"* he asked as he smiled. Such kindness and gentleness radiated in his voice. *"Oh no,"* I thought. *"What if it's not gone?"*

*"Would you please check yourself"* he asked again. *"Okay Becky, you have got to check yourself. You came up here so just check it,"* I

thought to myself. My hand slowly moved to my right breast. I pressed on the spot where the large painful quarter size lump had been for many months. My mouth opened in shock and surprise. *"It's gone,"* I declared. I stood stunned and shocked. Thoughts whirled quickly through my mind. *"It is really gone. There is no pain. How can this be? It is gone!"* I looked over at the gentle sweet smile of the pastor and knew at that moment I had received a miracle.

Many years later I began to realize that through this experience God was not only revealing to me that He was a God of love and hope, but that He would use situations in my life to expand my faith and trust in Him. He truly wanted to encourage me, to reveal the many fears in my thoughts and to help my unbelief.

Medicine, nutrition, exercise and miracles are some of the ways God bought healing to me, but I would soon learn there were still more.

## Electrical Waves of Healing

One of the more unusual manifestations of healing I experienced occurred late one Saturday evening about a year after the lump in my breast disappeared. It was a season when my body was once again in nearly continuous pain. The littlest bump or stumble while walking would set my body and muscles into excruciating pain. After completing dinner and the dishes, I turned quickly, tripped and fell into the kitchen cabinetry. I immediately declared *"Becky, you are ok. You are not going to be hurt by this!"* I rebuked any injury and professed my healing by His stripes and continued to complete my kitchen cleaning. However, within 15 minutes, muscle spasms and pain began to form in my back. The pain ran down my right leg. I began to panic and ask my husband where we could go to get me some relief. It was 9pm and all medical clinics were closed. *"Oh God,"* I cried, *"Help me please, I don't know if I can take these episodes of pain anymore. Please help me."*

Richard calmed me down and asked to pray for me. My back hurt so badly I lay down on the floor and closed my eyes. He began to pray in the Spirit and I tried to rest my body as I again asked God to please, help me. I was so tired of the many years of continual pain. I was frustrated and discouraged.

As Richard continued to pray, I began to feel a tingling in my toes. *"Oh no,"* I thought, *"My leg is going numb."* I also began to feel tingling in my leg. I realized this sensation was different from the feeling of numbness. This felt like my toes were in an electrical socket. The vibrating electricity intensified like a scanner moving across my body. The electricity began to move and flow. What was happening to me? It became a wave of electricity that was moving from my toes up to my knees, then slowly to my thighs, past my waist and up to my shoulders. The wave of electricity slowly continued up to my chin. My lips began to tingle with the sensation of electricity as it continued to the top of my head. As I lay there, now fascinated by what was happening to me, I wondered if it would stop. It continued from the top of my head back down to my toes. This peaceful wave of electricity flowed over me many times. Then the tingling slowly diminished. I was stunned by this event. I slowly sat up and stood to my feet. The pain in my body was gone. My anxiety was gone and I sensed an inward peace that all was well.

I have not experienced this amazing sense of glory and healing since that night and it did not permanently heal and restore my body. Nevertheless, I celebrated the next few days without pain. My search for healing continued, but I had experienced a visitation of His healing touch that night that left me changed and strengthened. God allowed me to see how much He cares about our hurts and pains. Jesus chose the Cross so that we could experience healing in every area of our lives. Whether He comes to us with a physical experience like I had in this case, or He comes to renew our minds or heal our souls — His desire is to touch us and see us healed and free. He comes to reveal His nature and character of Love (1 John 4:8).

# Prayer of Faith - Anointing with Oil and Laying on of Hands

There have been numerous times I have asked for prayer in my spiritual community and received physical healing by being anointed with oil or the touch of a Saint's hand. We are encouraged in James 5:14-15 to pray for one another. "Is anyone among you sick? Let him call for the elders of the church, and let them pray over him, anointing him with oil in the name of the Lord." Then we may exercise our faith in prayer so "that the prayer offered in faith will restore the one who is sick, and the Lord will raise him up, and if he has committed sins, they will be forgiven him."

Once during a three day seminar in 2006 I was having unbearable lower back and hip pain. I wanted to hear the speaker Randi Lechner[6], and so I told my body we were going to the meeting. Of course when you attend a conference you do a lot of sitting. Halfway through the first day I found myself needing to stand. It was embarrassing to think of going to the back of the room and standing all day against the wall, but I felt I had no choice. The chronic pain was not leaving. Randi continued to speak for some time and I continued to stand with my back against a wall for support. During a break, he came over to ask me if I was in pain. I acknowledged my predicament and he asked if he could pray for me. He placed his hand upon my shoulder and began to ask God to release healing to my body. After his prayer, he asked me how I felt. The pain was still there. Randi continued to pray and encourage me. *"Now, how do you feel?"* he asked. I bent over and realized the pain had vanished. I was able to sit for the next two full days without any pain or discomfort in my back or hip. Months later I was still working and walking without debilitating pain.

## Communion

There are theologians and traditions in some denominations

who believe that physical healing only operated in the early church. Others believe when taking communion that the bread and wine becomes the actual body and blood of Christ. As stated earlier, this book has not been written to debate differing theological points of view. Receiving communion has greatly impacted my life and the purpose of this book is to simply share my personal experiences with healing and the various paths you may choose to walk. I leave it to you Beloved, to search and knock on the doors you sense are for you. Communion has been one of the many doors of healing where I have received strength and our Master's touch.

When taking communion we often share the importance of self-examination. If we find we have un-forgiveness, anger, resentment, bitterness, criticalness or judgments; we first forgive others, forgive ourselves, and then give God our concerns and ask Him to forgive us. It is important to make peace with those in our spiritual families before receiving the elements.

Paul addressed the Corinthians expressing his concerned that many were sick. In 1 Corinthians 11:28-30 he said: "But let a man examine himself, and so let him eat of the bread and drink of the cup. For he who eats and drinks, eats and drinks judgment (condemnation) to himself, if he does not judge (discern) the body rightly. For this reason many among you are weak and sick, and a number sleep." It is good to remember Holy Spirit resides within each member of God's Body. When we criticize or degrade a brother or sister in Christ, we offend God. We must be careful to rightly discern and honor God's family, so we do not open ourselves to illness, disease, or even death.

How merciful of God to give us such a beautiful process to not only identify and remember Christ's suffering; but to also have a time when we can sit with Him and resolve issues of un-forgiveness in our hearts. It is important to God that we forgive. He gave us the Lord's Prayer reminding us to forgive so He can forgive us. In Matthew chapter 18, Peter came to Jesus and asked how often he was to forgive. Jesus responded to Peter to forgive not just seven times, but seventy times seven. As He continued, He compared the kingdom of heaven to a certain king who was settling accounts with his slaves. One of the slaves was unable to pay his account so he cried out for mercy from his lord. The lord responded with compassion and forgave him his debt. Now when the slave went out and found one of his fellow slaves who owed him, he assaulted him and demanded that he be paid immediately. His fellow slave fell down and also begged for mercy and patience saying he would repay as soon as he could. However the slave who had been forgiven by the lord, refused to forgive his fellow slave. The lord heard of this event and called the slave back to say, "Should you have not had mercy on your fellow slave, even as I had mercy on you?" Now with anger the lord handed him over to the torturers until he could repay all of his debt. A sobering admonition and finish to Jesus' parable is found in verse 35: "So shall My heavenly Father also do to you, if each of you does not forgive his brother from your heart."

Forgiveness is a key to healing. It brings health and deliverance. It is important we rightly discern the Spirit of God in each member of His Body. If we lose sight of this truth and entertain animosity toward others instead of extending forgiveness and peace, we may find ourselves battling challenges or disease.

Sometimes it is just hard to forgive. The hurts and wounds are so deep we don't know how to let go. In those times, I have found God to be my friend as I told Him how difficult it was to let go of the pain. I felt it wasn't fair to forgive someone and let them off the hook when they had hurt me so deeply. He gently reminded me of these Scriptures and asked me to let Him help. *"Father, please forgive me for holding this resentment, and help me forgive. I just can't seem to get rid of this pain."* As I gave up trying to make forgiveness happen by myself, in a short time the pain was more bearable and before long forgiveness had been birthed in my heart. *"I forgive them Lord."* Peace was restored to me and joy returned.

Forgiveness is also a key to grace. As we recognize more fully the sin we have entertained and the total cleansing work of the Cross in our own lives, we are able to extend grace and mercy to others as well as to ourselves. Giving grace and forgiveness brings freedom and healing to all. Taking the time for reflection and self-examination can birth greater compassion and mercy.

Receiving communion brings many benefits. We are able to bring our pain and un-forgiveness as well as our sorrow to Him. We are reminded of the importance of preferring and blessing others, and we continue to receive His love and healing touch as we renew His covenant of peace.

Healing comes in many ways; sometimes through a miracle and sometimes through the simple act of forgiveness. As you choose to take communion, take time for God to reveal any hidden issues in your heart. As you choose to ask Him for forgiveness and release the pain to Him, allow His river of life and forgiveness to flow to you.

## Gifts of the Spirit

The apostle Paul in 1 Corinthians 12:4-12 instructed the church of Corinth in their understanding of spiritual gifts. He shared that there are a variety of gifts but the same Spirit, just as there are varieties of ministries but the same Lord. Each ministry works in a different way, but it is the same God who makes them work through His people. Each person is given the expression of the Spirit for the good of all mankind. Verse eight identifies the gifts given through Holy Spirit. They include: word of wisdom, word of knowledge, gift of faith, gifts of healing, working of miracles and the gift of prophecy, discerning of spirits, tongues and interpretation of tongues. Holy Spirit distributes these gifts to each person as He wills for the encouragement and edification of everyone.

Controversy abounds concerning these spiritual gifts. All things in life can be misused or perverted, but I have found these precious gifts to be important and crucial in various seasons of my life. The gift of prophecy as well as the word of wisdom, both of which give insight into possible future events, has been given to

Richard and me many times birthing encouragement and hope, particularly when we felt lost and alone. Healing was manifested through the word of knowledge when I was healed of the breast lump which we discussed earlier. Another experience came unexpectedly one night in a meeting in January of 2007, when a speaker[7] paused and said: *"God is healing leaky bladders right now. If you have this situation please stand up for prayer."* I had been running to the bathroom with small accidents for months and it seemed to be worsening. Each morning began with a sprint from my bed hoping to avoid an accident. I had been asking God to help me understand what was happening and to please heal me. It had not dawned on me that this could be a leaky bladder, but when she spoke the phrase my thoughts said, *"Yes, that's me."* I stood for prayer and went home that night hoping that in the morning I would see a change. I woke up and made my way to the bathroom without incident. What thankfulness I felt. When one has been challenged by sickness or disease, little things often mean so much. How wonderful it was just to be able to walk to the bathroom in the morning without incident.

## Deliverance

Often when we hear the word deliverance we think of gruesome and vile images we have seen in the movies. I did too. So when it was suggested that I consider participating in a deliverance meeting I was not sure what I would encounter. I learned that deliverance is nothing to fear. In my experiences of receiving ministry and prayer I have sensed peace, increased mind clarity and contentment without any bodies convulsing, gyrating or levitating.

If we believe the Bible is true, then we also understand that evil spirits still affect people as they did thousands of years ago. In the first chapter of Mark, Jesus healed Simon's mother-in-law and by the evening people were bringing to Him "all who were ill and those who were demon-possessed" (verses 30-32). The entire city had gathered at the door of Simon's home and throughout the night "Jesus healed many who were ill with various diseases, and cast out many demons; and He was not permitting the demons to speak, because they knew who He was" (verse 34). Jesus then continued through Galilee, preaching and expelling demons (verse 39).

Almost any missionary who has served in other countries will tell you of inconceivable manifestations of dark forces they have witnessed first hand. Actually, we have many manifestations in our land, but they are often explained away in scientific and psychological terminology which is more palatable and less offensive.

Demonic oppression can cause different levels of torment: physical, mental or emotional. This is a ministry within the Body of Christ that is often misunderstood, frequently receiving criticism and skepticism. It is actually a ministry based on repentance and forgiveness. What is the purpose of repentance? It is to bring change in our minds and in our lives. Repentance, like our salvation, comes from God through His grace. 2 Timothy 2:25 tells us "God may grant us repentance leading to the knowledge of the truth."

Un-confessed sin may also cause us to be afflicted by evil forces. Just saying the word "sin" can bring horrific, evil, dastardly acts or images into our mind, but actually sin simply means "to miss the mark." When we entertain any kind of unscriptural behavior we often open the door to oppression and hardship. We miss the mark. We read in Proverbs 5:22 that "his own iniquities will capture the wicked, and he will be held with the cords of sin." The word iniquity means to turn the shoulder from God or to choose to do things our own way. When we choose to live life on our own terms, we set ourselves up to be captured in our iniquity. Verse 23 instructs that we "die from lack of instruction and in the greatness of our folly we go astray."

The good news is God is a loving and merciful Father. James 2:13 encourages us that "mercy triumphs over judgment." So a true Godly sorrow brings us to true repentance, just as forgiving others allows us to receive forgiveness from God (Luke 11:4).

As God illuminates the depth of our depravity we begin to realize the great need for His mercy and deliverance. As we repent we are brought to salvation which brings us into life as stated in 2 Corinthians 7:10: "For the sorrow that is according to the will of God produces a repentance without regret, leading to salvation; but the sorrow of the world produces death." Remorse, a worldly sorrow, is felt when we get caught in the act; but Godly repentance carries the weight and understanding of our action and will restore us to Him.

Deliverance is another door to healing and freedom which is often overlooked. It is not a panacea for healing by itself, but when coupled with prayer and counsel there is usually freedom and life. The process of deliverance is to recognize our weakness, and through repentance and forgiveness, receive God's grace and liberation. 1 John 1:9 states that "If we confess our sins, He is faithful and righteous to forgive us our sins and to cleanse us from all unrighteousness." What a wonderful promise!

I have personally witnessed amazing life changes for those who have chosen to participate in this ministry by examining their lives and the ways they have possibly opened themselves up to oppression. There are those who do not believe demons are real. I can understand their resistance to this belief. However, because I have personally witnessed levitations and other demonic manifestations that have been described in Scripture, the realm of spiritual darkness has become quite real to me. Thus, I would encourage you to investigate this avenue of healing and decide for yourself if it is a door for you.[8]

## Can We Lose Our Healing?

Like everything in this world, things can change. Does our body heal itself from colds and flu? Yes, but we may get over the cold and return to health, only to contact another cold and go through the healing cycle again. Re-occurrences of disease and sickness do happen. People experience repeated health challenges in the medical arena. Responding to life with continued stress or anxiety, continuing to harbor anger or un-forgiveness, disregarding nutritional laws or eliminating exercise in our activities, not feeding our spiritual needs through prayer and growing in the understanding of Scripture all can contribute to poor health. Receiving a healing or miracle does not make us immune to any sickness or disease. However, being touched by God does increase our faith and give encouragement that He is with us, helping and guiding us as we walk through life.

When we receive healing from God, we also receive an important assignment to maintain our new health and freedom. Studying Scripture and meditating on God's promises will help you conquer the old belief systems, mind sets, and attitudes that have hindered God from moving in your life. Watch and be vigilant concerning any un-forgiveness, guilt, shame, resentment, fear, or pride that may manifest through daily experiences. Be attentive as you identify harmful thoughts or emotions, and then begin to deal with them through repentance and forgiveness. We find in 2 Corinthians 10:5 instructions "to take every thought captive." Attacking fear and unbelief, doubt, anger, rejection, criticalness, or judgmental attitudes will strengthen your mind as well as your body. It is our responsibility to be watchful as we maintain and walk in His blessings.

Scripture encourages us in James 4:7 to "Submit therefore to God. Resist the devil and he will flee from you." When we daily submit ourselves to God, we receive His strength and power which helps us to resist the trials and thoughts that may cause us to fall.

Speaking Scriptures out loud gives us strength as we declare God's promises and testify to what Jesus has done for us through the Cross. And as you develop the time you spend with Him, talking and sharing, you will find He will gently speak to you in your thoughts, guiding you and giving you clarity and direction.

There is such diversity and creativity in healing. God is continually revealing Himself to us as He releases knowledge and understanding concerning His precepts and statutes. He moves through the research scientist who develops new medical procedures and medications, and He displays Himself in those who study herbs and natural foods in our world that bring strength and health. He teaches us the benefits of His dietary laws in Scripture; and He instructs us in the importance of forgiveness and repentance, as well as the benefits of exercise and understanding His covenant. Even with Scriptures and all the knowledge and resources available in this day, healing can still be elusive. So, He teaches us to seek the Healer and not just the healing.

Paul spoke to the church at Philippi, in chapter three of the book of Philippians, teaching them about the goal of life. He exhorted them to rejoice in the Lord and "to press on toward the goal for the prize of the upward call or vocation of God," learning to live with an understanding and attitude of the Cross of Christ. God never shares in Scripture that our lives will be idyllic, without pain or incident, albeit we would all love for life to be that way. His promises are that He will always love us, never forsake us, be with us and guide us, encourage and support us as we sojourn through this world in preparation for our heavenly home.

There have been seasons when I have found great comfort and strength in praying and meditating on this prayer daily:

*"Father, thank You for healing me and for breathing life back into my body, my soul and my spirit. Jesus, I thank You for Your work on the Cross and that I am healed by the stripes You bore on Your back for me. I thank You that the blood You shed on the Cross protects me and has cleansed me from all defilement, human and demonic. You live within me and I am a temple of the Holy Spirit. Every cell in this body, I now command you to function properly and line up with God's written word and spoken word. Every unclean spirit of infirmity you must leave now and not return in Jesus' name. God has given me authority to cancel your assignment. I will no longer listen to your lies."*

## Negative Beliefs

I don't know if I believe God wants to heal me.
I have seen God heal others, but I don't know if He would want
    to heal me.
I'm just emotional. He can't help me with that.
Jesus doesn't heal anymore. That was only in the Bible.

## Scriptural Truths

Jesus bore the stripes of suffering on his back so I might be healed.
God's desire is for me to be in health and have my soul prosper.
Jesus is the same yesterday, today and forever. He never changes
    and He forever heals.
Engaging in my intellect and over-thinking can hinder healing.

## Scripture Meditations: "It is written..."

3 John 1:2 — "Beloved, I wish above all things that you may prosper
    and be in health, even as your soul prospers."

Psalm 107:20 — "He sent his word, and healed them, and delivered
    them from their destruction."

Matthew 9:35 — "And Jesus went about all the cities and villages,
    teaching in their synagogues, and proclaiming the gospel of the
    kingdom, and healing every kind of disease and every kind of
    sickness."

Hebrews 13:8 — "Jesus Christ is the same yesterday and today, and
    forever."

Isaiah 53:5 — "But He was pierced through for our transgressions,

He was crushed for our iniquities; the chastening for our well-being fell upon Him, And by His scourging we are healed."

1 Peter 2:24 — "And He Himself bore our sins in His body on the cross, that we might die to sin and live to righteousness; for by His wounds you were healed."

Isaiah 54:17 — "No weapon that is formed against you shall prosper; and every tongue that shall rise against you in judgment you shall condemn. This is the heritage of the servants of the Lord, and their vindication is of me, declares the Lord."

## Reflections...

_____

_____

_____

_____

_____

_____

_____

_____

_____

_____

_____

_____

_____

_____

# 9
# WHY DO I STILL HURT?

Even though I experienced a wonderful miracle and the lump had miraculously disappeared from my breast, muscle pain and spasms continued to reoccur in my back, neck and shoulders. Arthritic pain in my joints would make it difficult for me to stand or walk. One evening, while I once again was telling the Lord how confused I was and that I was wondering what I had done to deserve this terrible pain, I asked Him how I was going to get out of this situation? I was losing hope. Was I ever going to feel healthy or normal again? How are you going to heal me, Lord? I've tried everything. I heard this still quiet voice whisper in my mind, "Why should I heal you?" Hmmm, now that was a shocking and unexpected answer. I began to mediate and started the list of all the wonderful reasons why God should heal me: "Well, because You love me, because You say I am healed by Your stripes, because I asked You to heal me, because I want to be able to take care of my child and husband, I want to run again and I want to be able to clean my house and work my job without pain and pay my bills, because I am tired of the pain, because You are merciful." As I continued the list I began to hear myself speaking and realized all of the reasons I wanted to be healed were for me. I was struck at the self-centeredness of my petitions.

I sat quietly for a moment and then asked the question, "Why, God, would You want to heal me?" In the stillness of that moment I heard a gentle small voice ask a question that would change my paradigm and begin to renew my mind and heart. *"If I heal you, will you serve Me?"* It had never even entered my mind that God might desire or require something of me. I had perceived that God was like a candy store and I could just go in and tell Him what I needed and He would give it to me. God had always been someone up in the sky looking down on me to see if I was being good or bad. It was my belief that if I was good, He would be good to me and like me. I tried to please Him, always seeming to fail. It was a sobering moment for me when I realized He desired something of me. It took me a number of days to reflect before answering the question. One would think I would have jumped at that moment to say, "Yes, Lord – I will serve You, now heal me." But in not being able to answer immediately, I became very aware of my love for my own life and my love for my own gain. I began to see my rebellion to Him in desiring to do what I wanted to do, when I wanted to do it. I really didn't want someone to tell me what to do or put a crimp in my plans. I just wanted Him to be good to me and bless me. I just wanted to be healed so I could do what I wanted to do. Days later, I was finally able to say: "Lord, I surrender my life and my desires to You and I choose to serve you as You wish. Please heal me Lord, and have mercy on me and give me the strength to commit to You and serve You."

My own choices and thoughts in life had brought me to this place of surrender. Everything I had tried to accomplish on my own and every way I tried to be whole had been met with little success. I had given my heart to God at the tender age of four, but I did not realize there would come a time He would visit me to ask me to align myself with His purposes and plans. I would find out later I had now chosen to step onto the road of transformation and restoration. He would begin to renew my mind. I was entering a purifying process I knew little about. I had surrendered myself to Him and now He would begin the covenant exchange process of changing me into His likeness.

## Taking the Ax to the Root

In the early 1980's I was privileged to attend a meeting with Dick Mills.[9] I wanted all of God and was trying to figure out how to know Him. In this particular meeting Dick Mills addressed detrimental characteristics in our lineage and in ourselves that we needed God to address and change. He suggested we make a list of characteristics we did not particularly like in ourselves. Some of mine included: pride, fear, anger, manipulation, control, resentment, and un-forgiveness. Not a pretty list. As I wrote them down, I kept my paper close to me so others would not see what was really inside me. It was embarrassing and shaming to think I loved God and still had these kinds of behaviors in my life. How in the world could I get rid of these things? Where did they come from?

Dick Mills then encouraged us with Luke 3:9, "And also the axe is already laid at the root of the trees; every tree therefore that does not bear good fruit is cut down and thrown into the fire." I quietly walked up to the altar and placed these unwanted characteristics at the feet of Christ and asked Him for His help. At the time I didn't have a clue how God was going to help me with these behaviors I did not like in myself. Later I would realize I was submitting myself to God for His correction, as I asked Him to make me more like Him. What I did not know was this exchange or transformation process would "cause" me to mature through life experiences, including trials, rejection, challenges, hurt, pain and even illness.

## Negative Beliefs

I am a happy person and I don't have any problems.
I never get angry, I just get hurt.
I never control anyone or any situation.
If I smile and be quiet my life will be peaceful.
They hurt me so it is all right for me to hurt them.
I don't want or need to forgive them.
I am not going to react. I'll just push this hurt down and it will go away.
I don't have a right to express my opinion.
Just get over it.
If people like me, then I am successful.

## Scriptural Truth

Jesus is the healer of my soul's diseases.

Forgiving others allows me to be forgiven by God.

Jesus does not judge or condemn. He asks me to not judge or condemn also.

Jesus is well acquainted with my sorrows and disappointments.

Holding onto pain or choosing denial will only prolong my suffering.

God desires for my mind to be renewed so I may have emotional and physical health.

## Scripture Meditations: "It is written...."

Revelation 12:11 — "And they overcame him (satan) because of the blood of the Lamb and because of the word of their testimony, and they did not love their life even to death."

Isaiah 48:10 — "Behold, I have refined you, but not as silver; I have tested you in the furnace of affliction."

2 Corinthians 4:17-18 — "For momentary, light affliction is producing for us an eternal weight of glory far beyond all comparison. While we look not at the things which are seen, but at the things which are not seen; for the things which are seen are temporal, but the things which are not seen are eternal."

Philippians 3:10-11 — "That I may know Him, and the power of His resurrection and the fellowship of His sufferings, being conformed to His death, in order that I may attain to the resurrection from the dead."

Romans 12:2 — "And do not be conformed to this world, but be transformed by the renewing of your mind, that you may prove what the will of God is, that which is good and acceptable and perfect."

2 Corinthians 3:18 — "But we all, with unveiled face beholding as in a mirror the glory of the Lord, are being transformed into the same image from glory to glory, just as from the Lord, the Spirit."

## Reflections...

# 10
# WHAT DID I DO TO DESERVE THIS?

"*What did I do to deserve this?*" said my friend as we sat in my living room. "*I don't understand what I did in my life to end up like this?*" She had come to discuss with me the challenges she faced and her need for healing. She was battling a prolonged illness and had lost a great deal of money. In her affliction, she had looked to God as the source of her pain. God was the enemy. She believed He was angry with her and had chosen to punish her. In her eyes, God had left her. Having known this person for many years I was somewhat stunned by her confession. This had been a strong active individual who I had watched over the years exhibit great trust and faith in God.

I was quickly taken back to my own misperceptions and beliefs I developed about God. There were years of crying out to Him wondering what I had done wrong or what I needed to do for Him to love me enough to touch me and take away challenges and pain in my life. It had taken me years to process His love and His desire to heal me. It was now evident my friend was experiencing her own personal trials while searching for God's acceptance. *Did she have an understanding of God's principles and precepts?* Even though she was a leader in the spiritual community I attended, there were times I had observed her being critical, controlling and judgmental. She occasionally found comfort in another's pain. She attended church regularly and loved to talk about God, but I had never really observed her studying Scripture or discussing His principles or statutes. She knew God from a distance but had never really developed a personal relationship with Him.

Scripture tells us that "My people perish for lack of knowledge" (Hosea 4:6). When we choose a life of seeking pleasures or making idols instead of learning to know and understand God and His ways, we often find ourselves confused and alone when adversity comes. For the majority of my life I knew about God and loved Him. I thought He was a good God and would not let anything happen to me. I tried to be a good girl and say my prayers every night. I saved myself for marriage. To me this was the extent of my relationship. I would read the Bible periodically, but quickly put it down as boring or too difficult to understand. I would look at it on my desk and think I needed to study, but I would quickly become distracted and decide I just didn't have the time. So when adversity came, beginning with the night of the accident, I began a journey of confusion and misperception ultimately ending with the assumption that God hated me and was out to get me. If this was the God I loved and He would treat me like this, then I didn't know if I wanted much to do with Him anymore. And so, I ended up bitter and angry with everything and everyone. I worked hard and kept busy denying my anger and disappointment, which was unconsciously directed at God.

I was living a life of denial. I was having selective hearing about the things of God. I wanted to hear He was loving and forgiving and merciful and full of grace – which He is and more. But I really didn't want to hear or study about His statutes or commandments. I didn't want to hear of my responsibilities in this relationship with Him or the character He was asking me to develop. By the year 2000, after years of enduring pain and trying every secular medical approach to healing I could find, I finally gave up and knew it was time to talk with God about what was happening to me and why I continued in such excruciating and disabling pain. I was finally really ready to listen. What I learned and experienced in the next few years was not a pretty picture. God exposed many dark things in my heart, but His revelation began to bring clarity and understanding to my journey.

One of the first revelations in my quest for truth and healing was found in the writings of John and Paula Sanford of Elijah House.[10] God had other laws than the Ten Commandments. I was amazed and suddenly very aware I had breached each one of these principles in my life. Could this possibly be one reason I was unable to receive healing?

May I share with you these principles that were life-changing for me? They have helped me to understand my breach with God and how to begin to walk toward healing and freedom.

---

*1) "Honor your father and mother, as the Lord your God has commanded you, that your days may be prolonged, and that it may go well with you on the Land which the Lord your God gives you" (Deuteronomy 5:16).*

---

It was time to look at myself and the anger and resentment that over the years had built up toward my parents. I became aware that even with amazing parents it is still possible to develop unhealthy attitudes and perceptions. As we develop and mature into adulthood, it is not unusual in any family to have conflict between what parents think is good and acceptable and what a child believes to be appropriate. Judgments and criticisms often result from the conflict and may become rooted in our heart. We become angry or resentful over things our parents did or did not say. Beliefs develop and take root in our thought life, from our perceptions that our parents hurt, controlled, or wounded us. Most of the time our parents have our best interest at heart; however, there are those who have suffered very real physical or emotional abuse. Sometimes we feel we have a "right" to be angry or upset with events in our childhood; nevertheless, God is asking us to give our pain and hurt to Him at the Cross and let Him help us eradicate it so we can respect and honor our mothers and fathers. It is important to come to the understanding our parents did their best with what was given to them. We are asked to extend mercy and grace to them as God has to us. If we choose to continue to dishonor them or disrespect them by our thoughts, words, or deeds, it is clear in this verse that we will open the doors to trouble and difficulties in our own lives.

2) *"Do not judge lest you be judged. For in the way you judge, you will be judged; and by your standard of measure, it will be measured to you" (Matthew 7:1-2).*

3) *"Therefore you are without excuse, every man of you who passes judgment, for in that you judge another, you condemn yourself; for you who judge practice the same things" (Romans 2:1).*

Life is full of judgments. Little thoughts flood through our minds throughout each day. *"Look at her! I would never do that. What is he doing? Who do they think they are? I sure wouldn't say that."* Trash talk is common among our young people. Criticizing others and exalting ourselves is constantly being projected on sitcoms and other media. People are judged by where they live, what they say, where they go to school, what they wear, what they look like, how they behave, or what car they drive. How weary God must be hearing our thoughts and criticalness toward one another. Even as children at very early ages, we may have said, *"I'm never going to be like that,"* or *"I hope I'm not like that when I grow up."* These are judgments whether we say them or think them, and when we judge others we will begin to experience those very same judgments in our lives at some point. It is not unusual within any generation to hear friends or siblings say for example: *"I hoped I would not hoard things and become a pack rat like my dad, but I find myself doing the same thing he did when I was young. I just couldn't stand it."* In reality, a judgment was made in their youth. It may take years for the fruit to be observed, but it will usually return in some form to the one who made it.

I have made so many judgments in my life it would take a book to list them all. I continue daily to ask Holy Spirit to reveal my judgments so I may repent, learn from them and be free from their destruction. If healing has eluded you, I would suggest you ask God to reveal any judgments or criticisms you may have made at one time or another. Memories, thoughts, or pictures in your mind will begin to appear. Take time to reflect on these events. Consider if they are true. If they are, share them with God and ask for His forgiveness. When we give these judgments to Him and ask Him to put them to death in our lives, He will.

If you at this moment are thinking of judgments you have made and your healing has eluded you, would you choose to pray this prayer with me? And as additional judgments are revealed to you, just continue to submit this prayer to Him.

---

*"Father, I ask You to forgive me for my judgment of _____. I forgive _____ for what they said/did to me. I am sorry for what I said and thought. I forgive myself Lord for not submitting to your statute. I give this judgment to You Father, and I ask You to put it to death at Your Cross. Now, please renew a right spirit within me and a pure heart. Thank you for Your love, Your mercy, and Your forgiveness."*

---

I first heard this next law or principle as a little girl watching Oral Roberts on television during his healing crusades. He often spoke regarding the law of sowing and reaping. I understood this principle in my finances but for some reason I was unable to see its importance in other aspects of my life.

---

*4) "Do not be deceived, God is not mocked; for whatever a man sows, this he will also reap. For the one who sows to his own flesh shall from the flesh reap corruption, but the one who sows to the Spirit shall from the Spirit reap eternal life" (Galatians 6:7-8).*

---

As I asked God for truth concerning this law, I began to realize the extent of the breaches I had made once again. I remembered the numerous times in dealing with people I chose legalism and judgment instead of mercy or grace. I had extended criticism instead of love; correction instead of support. I had placed impossible expectations on others. By not recognizing and implementing yet another law of God in my life, was I once again reaping the very things I had sown? When others would hurt me did I pray *"Father forgive them for they know not what they do"*, or did I hope for revenge and correction so they would know how it felt to be hurt? Perfection was the subliminal idol in my life. The world teaches us that perfectionism is a noble goal, so I learned to place high expectations on myself and others. I thought, *"If I'm trying to be perfect and responsible, why shouldn't everyone else have to be perfect and responsible too? Why can't people just be like me?"*

My eyes were being opened to the many years God extended great mercy and grace to me, but in my self-centeredness and my desire for fairness I misplaced the need for mercy and forgiveness to others. In not being able to forgive in my life, I now realized I tied God's hands and He was unable to forgive me. I was the one keeping me from freedom and blessing. Even the Lord's Prayer (Matthew 6:12) instructed me to "forgive us our trespasses as we forgive those who have trespassed against us." I was seeing more clearly now. "Do unto others as you would have them do unto you" (Matthew 7:12). "Take the log out of your own eye and then you will see clearly to take out the speck in your brothers" (Luke 6:42). *"Oh Father, I have held on to so much pain, bitterness and un-forgiveness. In this pain I have been angry at You and thought You didn't want me to be healed. I have been unable to see that in my ignorance I have breached Your laws and brought judgment upon myself. I now see that Your laws and Your correction are good for me. I see clearly how much You love me and how You have set boundaries about me for my protection and well being."* My lack of understanding of the ways of God and His Scriptures, laws, principles and statutes left me vulnerable. You see God is just and therefore is unable to breach His own law. So if I break a law, He is not able to say *"Oh whatever....I'll help you out of this again."* If we do not recognize our breach or sin and repent, God has no recourse in the matter. Proverbs 28:13 reminds us: "He who conceals his transgressions will not prosper, but he who confesses and forsakes them will find compassion." In my sin I chose to remove myself from His covering and protection. He does not negate or override His own law (2 Timothy 2:13). We deceive ourselves to think otherwise. But He has graciously made a way for us to be reinstated to right standing with Him, simply by repenting of our deed and asking His forgiveness. What amazing grace and mercy!

As we submit ourselves to God and allow Him to reveal our error, He is able to help renew our minds. He assists us in His beautiful process of transformation, slowly changing us into His likeness. Now, looking back, I can see His powerful hand upon my life working each day to develop my character through the work of the Holy Spirit; showing me my error, correcting me and sharing His truth so I can grow up and mature in Him. This is the process of transformation. This is His process of renewing our mind, our thoughts, beliefs and perceptions so we can develop more of His character and have less of our flesh. "And do not be conformed to this world, but be transformed by the renewing of your mind, that you may prove what the will of God is, that which is good and acceptable and perfect" (Romans 12:2).

This life journey of transformation is challenging. We are presented with the choice of living our lives as we please, or surrendering ourselves to God, allowing Him to change us more into His image and likeness. There has been heartache, confusion, rejection, humiliation, loss, sickness, pain and suffering; but there has also been love, mercy, grace, freedom, peace, protection, provision, comfort, great joy and resurrection life.

Thankfully, through this process, I am not the same person who started this journey as a child and I'm still changing day by day through each life experience. The many years of chronic pain were very challenging, but I now see everything in my life has been used in His mighty hands to guide me into a greater understanding of His ways and His statutes. God has continually been at work conforming me into more of His image. David must have had this revelation too when he sang to the Lord, "It is good for me that I have been afflicted so I may learn your statutes" (Psalm 119:71).

No one wants to be in pain or be challenged by grave illness. I do not believe God willingly causes illness or pain in our lives to punish or correct us. He is a God of love and life. Scripture comforts us in the third chapter of Lamentations declaring that God's mercies are new every morning. Love and mercy are wonderful characteristics of His nature. We are encouraged to have hope in God because He is faithful and good. He does not afflict willingly. If grief must come in our lives, He will also accompany it with His compassion. His loving-kindness never ceases and we can put our hope in Him.

God wants to give His goodness and blessings to His children. If you have children in your own life, do you not also want them to be happy, healthy and flourish? Well, our Father has that very same nature. He loves to see us prosper, mature and be in health. However, we live in a fallen world. We have been given the responsibility of making personal choices. There are horrific things that happen to very good people and children every day. Some things we just can not explain. Scripture states "we see through a glass darkly" (1 Corinthians 13:12).

There are atmospheric conditions that cause storms and havoc on the earth. There are evil diseases that torment and destroy life. Does God sit up in the heavens and plan these things for our destruction? Is He an angry God who waits to catch us and punish us? Is He happy when we are hurt and in pain? Oh no! That is what demons want us to believe. In our life challenges, the enemy comes to whisper condemning thoughts in our mind – *"God did this to you. God let this happen to you. God doesn't care about you!"* The enemy knows if we turn our back from God we will choose to leave His covenant blessings. Demonic forces attempt to pick away at our trust and belief so we will throw away God's protection, His love and peace, and His promises. We choose life or death everyday in the decisions we make and the things we choose to focus on. Do we choose to focus on loss and pain today, or do we focus on hope and life? What we focus on in our life, we make room for each day.

God is mysterious and we don't always understand His ways or why some suffer so gravely here on earth. However, we can take encouragement in knowing that through the suffering, He is ever present working His plans and changing us into His glorious nature by our submission to His truths. "That in reference to your former manner of life, you lay aside the old self, which is being corrupted in accordance with the lusts of deceit, and that you be renewed in the spirit of your mind, and put on the new self, which in the likeness of God has been created in righteousness and holiness of the truth" (Ephesians 4:22-24).

## Negative Beliefs

God does not want me to be happy.
I have sinned and He will never forgive me.
I will pay for my mistake for the rest of my life.
God likes to punish me and show me He is the boss.
I will never forgive them for what they did to me.
God doesn't care what happens to me.
Where was God when I was hurting so badly?

## Scriptural Truths

When I forgive others, God is able to forgive me.
When I repent of my sin, God takes it to the sea of forgetfulness and never remembers it again.
God knew me before the foundation of the earth and He has plans and cares for me.
God desires that I rest under His wings, so He can protect and watch over me.
All negative emotions need to be resolved because they will manifest sooner or later in some form.
I must learn to live with the criticism and judgment in this world.

## Scripture Meditations: "It is written..."

Isaiah 59:1 — "Behold, the Lord's hand is not so short that it cannot save; neither is His ear so dull that it cannot hear."

Psalm 46:1 — "God is our refuge and strength, a very present help in trouble."

Isaiah 54:17 — "No weapon that is formed against you shall prosper; and every tongue that shall rise against you in judgment you will condemn. This is the heritage of the servants of the Lord, and their vindication is from me, declares the Lord."

Isaiah 55:8-9 — "For My thoughts are not your thoughts, neither are your ways My ways, declares the Lord. For as the heavens are higher than the earth, so are My ways higher than your ways, and My thoughts than your thoughts."

Isaiah 55:11 — "So shall My word be which goes forth from My mouth; it shall not return to Me empty, without accomplishing what I desire, and without succeeding in the matter for which I sent it."

Jeremiah 29:11 — "For I know the plans I have for you, says the Lord, plans for welfare and not for calamity to give you a future and a hope."

Deuteronomy 5:16 — "Honor your father and mother, as the Lord your God has commanded you, that your days may be prolonged, and that it may go well with you on the Land which the Lord your God gives you."

Matthew 7:1-2 — "Do not judge lest you be judged. For in the way you judge, you will be judged; and by your standard of measure, it will be measured to you."

Romans 2:1 — "Therefore you are without excuse, every man of you who passes judgment, for in that you judge another, you condemn yourself; for you who judge practice the same things."

Galatians 6:7-8 — "Do not be deceived, God is not mocked; for whatever a man sows, this he will also reap. For the one who sows to his own flesh shall from the flesh reap corruption, but the one who sows to the Spirit shall from the Spirit reap eternal life."

John 3:17 — "For God did not send the Son into the world to judge the world, but that the world might be saved through Him."

2 Timothy 2:13 — "If we are faithless, He remains faithful; for He cannot deny Himself."

## Reflections...

# 11
# THE BREACH

Everyone seems to have at least one moment or memory in their lives when they felt betrayed, violated or traumatized. We attempt to process these events, but occasionally they are too painful or confusing to assimilate. As a result we may choose to disregard, ignore or deny the occurrence. However, later in life, our unresolved thoughts or memories may emerge.

My first experience with betrayal occurred in Indiana when I was quite young. We often visited my grandma and grandpa's house on the weekends. They lived on a small farm with a barn and cattle. I remember how much I enjoyed going up to the barn to pet the soft, fuzzy noses of the cows. It was also fun to wake up in the morning to the sounds of bacon sizzling in the skillet and the soft greeting of mourning doves. The delicious fragrance of breakfast would weave its way through their old farm house. We were far away from the cares of the city and our busy family schedule. Time seemed to stand still and I felt very safe and secure. I looked forward to our visits.

In my search for physical healing, my mind began to release experiences and emotions I had not allowed myself to think about, even back to early childhood. These events had been pressed down within me and long forgotten, until one day the movie began to roll in my mind. All of a sudden I was back on the farm.

When my family and I visited my grandpa and grandma, the kids would usually snuggle into their beds. I would sleep with grandma and my brothers would sleep with grandpa. Being a first grader, life was an adventure and everyday seemed to have something exciting to learn and experience. After a fun day on the farm, I put on my pajamas and jumped into my grandma's bed ready to snuggle in for the night. An older family friend jumped in with me before my grandmother came to bed. Being young and naïve, we giggled and talked, and he asked me to let him try something. Still in elementary himself, I do not believe this friend intended me any harm. Children can be curious about sexual activities. Not knowing what was ahead and being quite adventurous, I said *"Yes"*, giggling that a great game was in store. Quickly my expectations turned to disgust and confusion as I became upset and felt violated. Ugh! *"I'm going to tell my mom and dad,"* I proclaimed. He quickly asked me to not say anything and said he was sorry. That seemed sufficient to me, so I pressed down that moment in my little mind, grandmother came to bed and we finally all went to sleep.

Years later, as I questioned my parents about this memory, I found out this friend did go to my parents and tell them what had happened. He was corrected and my parents chose not to discuss or bring up the encounter again with me or with him. Their knowledge of child development supported the belief I was quite young and would not remember it. My experience became a family secret. I did not know at my young age how to mentally digest the encounter or to share with others about it, so I chose to bury it in my mind. I was unaware of the accompanying shame and guilt I experienced and accepted at that moment, and so I pushed down that unpleasant memory and locked it away in the small little compartment way back in the recesses of my mind.

When we experience a trauma in our life which is not resolved, it often has a way of hiding deep within our soul. Later in life we find the trauma begins to reveal itself in unexpected ways or behaviors. Difficult life experiences we suppress or deny can lead to various unhealthy responses, including physical illness in our bodies as well as emotional illness. For example, those who experience verbal or physical abuse may process the event with guilt and shame. *"I must have done something to provoke them. What did I do?"* In trying to mentally process the pain, they may place the responsibility for the event on themselves. *"I must deserve this. It's my fault."* These thoughts are not true. A person who has been verbally or physically abused is not responsible for the choices or actions of another person.

Hearing horror stories of friends' and family members' pregnancies and births, along with my unsettling and shameful introduction to sexual activity, I began to say to my family and friends that I never wanted to get married and I never wanted children. The subconscious memory of the event was beginning to manifest itself in lifestyle choices. In making these vows I was assuring myself unpleasant experiences would never, ever happen to me again.

The secret became a hidden and forgotten memory as I grew up, fell in love and married. I resolved with my husband we would not have children, but I was unable to pinpoint the reason for my choice. I just knew I did not want to become pregnant or have children. I threw myself into my career which was to be the emphasis of my life. Richard shared he was indifferent concerning children, so I seemed to be able to keep some control over my life and suppress the fear of childbirth and other unresolved thoughts.

## The Life Changing Choice

One afternoon in the spring of 1974, while sitting at lunch, I shared I had been feeling rather nauseated with a headache for a number of days. The secretary shrieked *"Oh, it sounds like you are pregnant!"* She was excited, but panic arose inside of me. I tried to keep my composure as I said, *"Oh, I'm sure I'm not expecting."* The rest of the day I could not concentrate on my work. *"What if I am? Oh no, this could not happen."* Fear rose within me as my heart pounded in my ears. I immediately was tested and waited for the results. *"Oh please, no, I can't do this!"* The call came. The results were positive. My panic increased and I began to hyperventilate. *"Calm down and think. What do I do?"* My husband came home and I shared the news. I asked him what he thought I should do. He was still indifferent and said, *"Do whatever you want to do."*

Abortion had just been legalized in Michigan. *"What was it like? Should I try this? Was it alright to do this? I have something growing inside me, but I don't think it is real yet. At least that's what the media says. How many months do I have before this thing growing inside of me becomes real or becomes human? What am I thinking? I think this is my baby or child, and yet, it just can't be. Is it even alive? It is not supposed to be there. This is not really happening. I didn't plan this."* I was now out of control. Panic and fear overwhelmed me. All I could think about was somehow stopping and controlling this situation. I was now not in control of my life. I was too ashamed to talk to anyone. *"How could I let this happen to me? My parents might be upset with me."* We just built our first new home and we were established in our jobs in the community. My life was going smoothly. Everything was supposed to be in order and going as planned. My thinking was now irrational. All I could focus on was the need for relief. I needed this to be resolved. I needed this to go away. I didn't know how to deal with this. This wasn't in my script for my life. I needed to keep this a secret. I didn't know what to do, but I could not trust anyone to help me. I talked with my husband and he said he didn't care. He said to "just do what I needed to do." His philosophy at the time was to let people make their own decisions. I couldn't even make a decision. How was I going to make this decision alone? If I made the wrong decision I would pay for it the rest of my life. What should I do?

This was all so surreal. There were no counselors to talk with and there was little information or truth available about the process of abortion at the time. In my irrational state, I thought for a few days and came to a panicked decision. I was too afraid to have children. I was afraid of the pain. Women were saying they were not giving drugs during delivery because natural childbirth was encouraged. I had just finished a degree in Exceptional Student Education. I had taken aspirins. *"What if they affected the embryo? What if this baby isn't 'normal'?"* I didn't know if I could handle that. *"How could this happen? I won't be able to work and we will lose our home."* All the reasons to abort came gushing through my mind as a massive wave of anxiety with *"I can't..., What if..., I ought to..., I should...,"* and *"I shouldn't."* I felt emotionally paralyzed.

The appointment was made. We drove to Michigan for the weekend to have the procedure. I felt apprehensive and afraid. Inside my mind I was totally alone. As I sat quietly in the waiting room my emotions were numbed. I stared at the stark white walls in perfect silence. I didn't feel anything but my heart racing and a voice inside my head saying *"Don't do this!"* They called my name. They prepared me for the procedure. Everything in me wanted to run. My heart was pounding. I had broken out in hives. *"Why didn't I run?"*

## Shock and Despair

As I lay on the table breathing heavily, upset, and tears in my eyes, the doctor stopped and asked, *"Are you sure you want to do this?"* The conviction in my spirit cried out, *"No"*, but the fear in my mind grew louder, clouding my thoughts and I answered *"Yes."* As I nodded to the doctor, I closed my eyes and detached myself from my body, unaware of anything around me. I suddenly sensed someone helping me up. They were saying something to me. I looked at the nurse's face trying to read her lips. Her voice sounded a thousand miles away. *"Are you ok? You can get up now. I will take you to the recovery room."* She took me to a small room like a large closet with two cots. *"Rest here and come out when you feel like it,"* she said.

I lay stunned and ashamed at what I had just experienced. I felt no relief, just great sadness. Staring up at the faded ceiling, I could hear faint activity outside the room. I could not think and I could not move. I couldn't even shed a tear. I just laid there staring at the ceiling, unable to process what I had just chosen to experience. I had entered a state of shock.

When we become traumatized, I am told "shock" is our body's way of protecting us and keeping us alive. Time stood still. I had no idea how long I lay on the cot in that room. A nurse finally came to me and asked if I felt alright and was ready to go.

She said I had been in recovery a long time. I said, *"Yes,"* as I stood up and began to walk out the door to Richard. As I was leaving, a 16 year old girl who had been placed in the room with me was chatting incessantly and telling me this was her second abortion. She seemed unaffected by her choice as she jumped off the recovery bed and bounded happily out the door before me. *"Oh, my dear God, what have I done?"* It was a question that was too overwhelming to even ponder.

The rest of the day and the ride back home was a blur. We stopped to get something to eat, but I didn't feel like eating. There was little conversation between us. A great sadness sat on my shoulders and I could no longer see color in the world or feel joy. The shock lasted for months. How was my mind going to process what had happened? *"Just process it like before. Just keep pushing it way down in your memory bank until it never comes up again. Try to forget it. Go on with life"* – and so I did. Over time I developed my own coping mechanisms to comfort me in the choice I had made. In fact, I became so comfortable with my decision; I opened up to a few about my procedure and encouraged those in the same state of panic to consider making the same choice. Of course if others made the same choice, my decision would seem more acceptable and my shame and guilt would not be as great. *"Everybody is doing it you know."* How deceitful the mind can be when we conjure up ways to resolve our conflicts and issues in ways that appear to vindicate us from any wrong doing. Throughout the years my mind would scream out, *"Oh God, why didn't I...? Why didn't You stop me? How could I do this? I am a murderer. You must hate me. You could never love me again."* And then I would once again push the thoughts back into the little compartment deep within my mind where I thought I could continue to lock them away and they wouldn't trouble me anymore. I didn't realize it, but shame began to grow in my heart. Hatred for myself and for my husband was watered daily by revisiting in my mind the horrid experience and the loss of our child.

When we make choices we regret they affect our lives and the lives of others. Sometimes we will be reminded of past events because God wants us to deal with the wound and resolve the pain attached to it. He isn't trying to bring up memories to torment us. He cares enough to reveal any darkness in our heart affecting us and everyone around us. God never leaves or forsakes us. He is always there loving us. I have learned His love is not conditioned on how wonderful we are. He is a Father of healing, redemption, restoration and amazing grace.

## Where Are You, God?

When I was in elementary school, I would often take the long way home by our church. I can remember many times quietly sneaking into the sanctuary hoping I would not get reprimanded by the Pastor and be asked to leave. I would sit there enjoying the silence and the peace I felt. I hoped I would hear God speak to me. I wanted to know Him and I wanted to talk with Him, but I didn't know how. By college my desire and thirst for knowing God became a futile goal. It was the seventies and confusion reigned as my generation began to challenge the establishment and their beliefs. The drug and sexual revolution permeated the airwaves and media. Riots and civil unrest were daily events throughout the nation. As I entered my first semester as a freshman at the university, I looked for college groups within our new church. I couldn't find them. There didn't seem to be any events or meetings available; but there were activities on campus and new friends to meet. So, I laid down my search for God and jumped into campus life.

During this time I did not have a strong relationship with God. I knelt and prayed before bed every night, but I prayed at a God somewhere up there in the sky that I hoped was hearing my prayers. I didn't really know if God heard me or if He even cared about me. He was not real to me and even after all the years of searching to find Him and to discover if He would talk to me, I could not sense His presence or hear His voice. I did not understand how God communicates with us. I began to rely on myself to be successful. I had a great need to be approved of by man. I began to make choices that would make me acceptable and make me feel valued and loved. I wanted to be beautiful. I wanted to be smart. I wanted to take charge of my life and become somebody. I wanted to be a star. I didn't realize during that freshman year I chose to walk in the world's ways.

Reflecting on this experience, I see more clearly each day how God was with me. The pounding heart beat and adrenaline rush, the voice in my head saying *"Don't do this, leave."* Even the doctor stopping one more time to make sure I wanted to proceed were all aspects of Holy Spirit trying to reach through my panic and fear. God had been talking to me, but I didn't know it. I didn't recognize His voice. I thought all those thoughts were just me. It would be a number of years before I would realize the depth of God's love for me and that He had always wanted to keep me from harm and poor choices. I would look back in my life and see that He desired a relationship with me and had been speaking to me.

## Secrets Carry Shame

This event was kept undercover for many years. Another secret added to my life. I was ashamed and fearful of telling my family what I had done. *Who could ever forgive me? Who could ever forget?* And it would be unthinkable to share this with someone in our church family or try to get counsel. Someone would find out. Someone would point the finger and look at me with disgust. I would not be accepted or loved.

Secrets can place us in darkness and isolate us. Shame often disables, keeping us from joy and freedom. It can take all our energy just to keep past memories hidden. We place a mask upon our face to hide the pain and shame we feel and to avoid the stares. We do what we must to be acceptable as we try to ignore or mask the dark things from within, hoping no one will ever find out who we really are. We work hard to conform to the world's standards making sure no one finds out we have made poor choices or entertained evil.

One year later in the spring of 1975, I was involved in the severe car crash discussed earlier. As I recovered from vertigo and a concussion at home, the questions reappeared. *"I thought everything was resolved. Was God punishing me now? I took a life and now I was a murderer."* Yes, I began to believe God was punishing me!

Physical trauma leaves its mark with bruises and scars which can be seen. Emotional trauma leaves scars also, but they are often hidden deep within our mind and soul, making them difficult to track and find the root.

My secrets became lost within me. Life continued to march on with rejections, betrayals, financial problems, guilt, shame and poor choices. With each event, I chose to place a mask upon my face. No one would ever know how I was hurt or what I had done. I was now safe again in the world. As long as I wore a smile, pleased people and told everyone I was fine, I would be safe and accepted.

Years passed with intermittent muscle pain and illness. In searching for relief, once again God revealed His truth. And with His encouragement, one by one, I approached each family member with the truth of my past. It was difficult and humiliating to share I was so human and could stoop so low, but it was also freeing. The news was out. I was not perfect. I had made a big mistake. I began to sense some relief. The stress and tension began to drain from my muscles. I was no longer working to hold on to my secret. I no longer feared being exposed or found out. I had adorned myself with the mask of perfection and in removing it, I was able to begin to find peace and contentment. I did not have to pretend any longer. I had made a poor choice. I had caused much pain to myself and others but I was still loved. I had learned a valuable lesson; that God's truths always bring freedom and life.

My mind wandered back to my childhood. I can remember the very place at the altar kneeling beside my grandmother, Sylvia, when I accepted Christ. I wanted to take communion like the adults and was told I couldn't unless I asked Jesus into my heart.

As a child of four, I innocently said *"Yes"* to Jesus. I immediately sensed this wave of warmth and joy I had never felt before. The atmosphere around me revealed bright light. Even being so young, I knew I was experiencing something holy and precious. I knew I was sensing God's presence and I fell in love with Him. I wanted to be in church all the time with my grandmother. My family gently teased me and called me "little Sylvia" as they watched me emulate my grandmother and her religious activities.

## Spiritual Performance Versus Spiritual Relationship

Up to entering college I attended church regularly. I enjoyed summer Bible camps in Junior High and continued my search for truth. Some laughed and compared me with my grandmother who was always attending or helping at her church community. It did not faze me because I knew in church I would get to experience His presence and His love. As much as I enjoyed being in that atmosphere, my heart began to wither as I entered college. I had heard a lot about God and His laws over the years and I had worked hard to try to be a good person and keep His statutes; but the withering that took place was the realization that I could never be good enough and never keep the "Thou shalts" that I was being told to keep. After the abortion I began to feel that I had failed God and myself. I just wasn't good enough and I would never be able to make God happy, so He would be pleased with me and love me. I had tried to keep His commandments and had failed. I had flunked the test: Thou shall not kill.

Looking back I realize some of the shock was the hatred and disgust I had for myself. I had sinned and let God down. I thought God would never be able to forgive me or love me again. I failed the test of being good. I separated myself from God by my disobedience. I would never be able to be good enough for Him and He would never look at me as His good little girl again. In reality, I failed to hear or understand I was not under the law anymore. I was now under the law of grace and God loved me unconditionally and would forgive me and restore me.

The law (Ten Commandments) in the Old Testament was given to show us we could never keep it. It prepared mankind to realize we needed a Savior who could redeem us from ourselves and our sin (or missing the mark). In church I was taught the law and about God, but I was not taught or instructed in His Spirit. I knew Jesus loved me and was my friend, but I did not understand He desired to have a relationship with me. I didn't know I could go to Him with questions and concerns and He would share His wisdom and truth with me. I did not know how to hear His voice or how to look for Him speaking in and around me. Not having a relationship with Him caused me to view God as a harsh, demanding Father in the sky who would give love to me and accept me if I was good. I tried so hard to be good but ultimately came to the reality I could never be good enough for God. I continued praying to Him but my heart had withered and my mind was confused with who God was. I began to entertain the question: *"Is God even real?"*

The performing, striving, false responsibilities, and good works for God I embraced were now exposed. Being unable to keep the law or earn God's love had unknowingly set me on a path of performance anxiety; however, finally accepting the mammoth realization of how I always strived and performed to get God to notice or affirm me, was a pivotal moment of truth. My striving and performing was in vain. He already loved me unconditionally! No matter what I did, He would never love me more or less. It would take many years to unwind the performance tentacles from my unbiblical beliefs, but I had new revelation and hope.

No matter what you have experienced in your life, there is a person who understands and identifies with your pain. His name is Jesus. Isaiah 53:3 tells us "He was despised and forsaken of men, a man of sorrows, and acquainted with grief; and like the one from whom men hide their face, He was despised and we did not esteem Him. Surely our griefs He Himself bore, and our sorrows He carried; yet we ourselves esteemed Him stricken, smitten of God and afflicted. But He was pierced through for our transgressions, He was crushed for our iniquities; the chastening for our well-being was upon Him, and by His scourging we are healed."

Ask Jesus to shed His light and truth on unresolved conflict or confusion in your life. Trust Him to guide you through circumstances He may desire to expose and heal. He will help you find peace. Jesus spoke in John 8:12: "I am the light of the world; he who follows Me shall not walk in the darkness, but shall have the light of life."

## Negative Beliefs

God likes me more when I am happy or when I am doing something special.

I am loved and accepted when I appear successful or have a special purpose.

God will never be able to forgive me.

I will never be able to forget this.

I can never forgive myself.

I will live with this for the rest of my life.

I am not allowed to make mistakes.

I work hard so I will not be criticized.

God will not like me if I feel angry.

When I am busy I am valued.

## Scriptural Truths

God forgives me and cleanses me from all I do that is wrong, when I repent.

God may convict me, but He does not come to condemn me.

God asks me to forgive myself and to love myself so I can love others.

God is merciful and when I ask Him to forgive me, He never brings up my sin again.

Forgiving myself and others is a precursor to my healing.

Even though God has not done anything which warrants our forgiving Him, misconceptions of His actions may need to be addressed for complete reconciliation.

Many illnesses are based on condemnation, shame and guilt. When I build altars to guilt and shame I am unable to rest in God's love and forgiveness.

## Scripture Meditations: "It is written..."

1 John 1:9 — "If we confess our sins, He is faithful and righteous to forgive us our sins and to cleanse us from all unrighteousness."

Psalm 103:10-12 — "He has not dealt with us according to our sins, nor rewarded us according to our iniquities, for as high as the heavens are above the earth, so great is His loving kindness toward those who fear Him."

2 Corinthians 5:17 — "Therefore if any man is in Christ, he is a new creature; the old things passed away; behold, new things have come."

John 5:24 — "Truly, truly, I say to you, he who hears My word, and believes Him who sent Me, has eternal life, and does not come into judgment, but has passed out of death into life."

Psalm 32:5 — "I acknowledged my sin to Thee, and my iniquity I did not hide: I said 'I will confess my transgressions to the Lord', and Thou didst forgive the guilt of my sin."

Hebrews 8:12 — "For I will be merciful to their iniquities, and I will remember their sins no more."

Ephesians 4:26 — "Be angry and yet do not sin; do not let the sun go down on your anger."

# Reflections...

# 12
# WHAT IS LOVE, JESUS?

An epiphany is a sudden moment when we discover truth. We search and pray hoping for understanding and revelation, often not knowing where it is or what it looks like. Sometimes it seems like the answer will never arrive. But if we patiently reflect and wait, the truth appears and we cry out "Eureka" knowing we have struck gold. When the light bulb turns on we receive wisdom and knowledge that can be significant and life-changing. These illuminated moments often become turning points in our life shifting us toward greater maturity and wholeness.

A major light bulb moment occurred in 2001, when after much reflection I acknowledged I didn't understand love. The truth was startling and bewildering.

I was finally able to admit I did not know how to love. I had never really truly loved. All of the expressions of my love now looked self-centered and tainted with my hidden motivations and needs. I thought I knew what love was. I thought I was experiencing love and expressing love in my relationships, but right there staring at me was the ugly truth. I didn't know how to love and I didn't even know what real love felt like or what it looked like. *"Oh God, I just want to know and feel love."* I fell to my knees in my bedroom as I let out a loud gut-wrenching roar. As I screamed and cried, I could hear the deep painful moaning being released from my inner being. The pain of the revelation was so intense and yet the joy of finally admitting the truth was so freeing.

Minutes passed by travailing and grieving the loss of a life of not understanding love. As I lay on the floor my mind began to accept the truth and I entered a peace and calm. My thoughts whirled back to a song written by Nancy Honeytree in the 1980's.

The melody and words began playing in my head. *"Tell me what love is Jesus....I'd really like to know. I'm beginning to doubt, all the things I've learned from the TV and the radio. Tell me what love is Jesus....how does it actually feel...are our feelings not quite so important, when love is real."*[11]

I knew this was a deep revelation from my Father. It was an answer to years of prayer and searching for the roots which had hindered me from peace. Now the revelation was manifest, but I had no clue what to do with it. My prayer came as a whisper: *"God, I don't know how to love! Father, help me to know what Your love is. How does Your love feel God? I'm confused and I'm tired of this human, painful, manipulative, self-serving love. I can't even feel real love. Teach me to love the way You love God! I can't live with the world's love anymore. I want to see people and love people the way You do."*

I had finally chosen to peek out from behind the curtain of denial and accept the disheartening revelation. Looking back at my life I could no longer refute I was a performer searching for love. I could now see how I allowed shame and self-hatred to mold me into a people-pleasing, self-loathing, manipulative, controlling, striving individual who carried bushels of false responsibilities and burdens while searching frantically for love and acceptance.

My hidden motivations and the various acts of performing were revealed in almost every area of my life. Their tentacles reached deep and wide. Days and months went by as I pondered the depth of my needs and self-centeredness. The pain of years wasted working and searching for a love to fill the hole in my heart was overwhelming. The only thing I knew to do at this point was to pray to God, *"Help me. I don't know how to unwind this behavior. It is too big for me Father. It is too ugly and I am sorry for believing these lies."*

Each day presented opportunities to address or resolve character issues and negative beliefs or paradigms I entertained in my life as truth. Additional insight would come giving me an abundance of homework as God was slowly renewing my mind.

In my search for truth, I began to realize why I was so confused.

The love I perceived and had been taught from the world was conditional. It was self-serving. It was about getting what I wanted. Life was supposed to be about what I could accomplish and what I could acquire. It was about people liking and admiring me. How many awards and "monuments" could I build to validate myself and to support my own self-importance? I had made myself an idol and the center of my universe. I had become a chameleon, trying to be what every person needed me to be so I could be liked, accepted and most importantly loved. Love to me was about me being exalted. I needed love from others to feel good about myself. I needed to feel valued and accepted. I had given the responsibility to others to tell me I was ok. People-pleasing had become one of my highest priorities in the hope I would be loved. Self-acceptance and love were trophies I was working to acquire and I was now too worn out to work for them anymore.

I recognized I couldn't make choices and decisions, because I didn't know who I really was, nor did I know who God was. I had needed other people to tell me who I needed to be, so I had never developed who I was. Inside I was still the little child trying to be accepted and approved of. I didn't even love myself. God revealed the self-hatred in my heart. I began to see the lies I had entertained. *"You'll never be good enough. You never do enough to be loved. Look how you have failed. Look at all the mistakes you have made. Your life is over. You're a mess. How could anyone love you?"*

In examining God's love (agape) in the Vine's Expository Dictionary, I found definitions in conflict with my idea of love. Their definition states God's love is the "attitude of God toward His son" (John 17:26). "Love can be known only from the actions it prompts. God's love is seen in the gift of His son" (1 John 4:9-10). Love seeks the welfare of all and works no ill to any. And in respect to *agapao* as used of God, it expresses the deep and constant love and interest of a perfect Being towards entirely unworthy objects, producing and fostering a reverential love in them towards the Giver, and a practical love towards those who are partakers of the same, and a desire to help others to seek the Giver."[12]

What a novel concept! *"You mean I don't have to work or perform for Your love God? You love me when I'm cranky, or sad, or mad or bad? You love me just because You created me?"* My perception of receiving love had always been about performing or being acceptable in some way. "Jesus loves me this I know, for the Bible tells me so" was a song I had sung since I was three, but I now was being awakened to a revelation of His true love. God's love is unfathomable. His love is more than our human brains can assimilate or comprehend. His love is strong and correcting, yet nurturing and comforting. It is not a love that He gives and takes away. He freely gives His love forever.

## God's Unconditional Love

God expresses His unconditional love to us in such subtle ways: by the air we breathe, the warmth of the sun shining on our face, the daily provision we receive, the laughter of our children or a call from a friend, the vibrant colors of the flowers and vegetation around us, the wind kissing our face, the smell of cookies fresh from the oven, the pay-check that pays our bills, and the birds chirping early in the morning. He shares His love by revealing His nature and character to us through our daily experiences. He teaches us His love in the Scriptures and through developing a relationship with Him. His love is in His correction which is always good. Every day is an experience of His love, His presence and His grace if we look for it. His love increases the desire within us to know Him more.

God's love is continually flowing from His heart to us. We sometimes have to look for it, but it is always there. The nature of His love is so poignantly described in 1 Corinthians 13:4-7: "Love is patient, love is kind, and is not jealous; love does not brag and is not arrogant, does not act unbecomingly; it does not seek its own, is not provoked, does not take into account a wrong suffered, does not rejoice in unrighteousness, but rejoices with the truth; bears all things, believes all things, hopes all things, endures all things."

It was a great relief to finally begin to rest in the knowledge and revelation that I was loved. I didn't have to feel alone or rejected anymore. I didn't have to try to perform or strive to achieve some great feat or become successful for God to love me. Even in my sin and iniquity God still loved me. I had been given a key of life knowing if no one else ever approved or loved me it didn't matter. I was really loved unconditionally by God, and there was nothing I could do or say to ever change His love for me. As I became conscious of God's love for me, I not only began to love myself, but I became aware of His love for others. I felt free.

If the world's love has let you down...if you are weary from performing or hoping to be loved...if you have a painful, aching hole in your heart that nothing can fill or you have committed what you believe to be an unpardonable sin, ask God to reveal His love to you. Ask Him to live inside of you and share His love with you. I have found Him always willing and waiting to reveal Himself and His love. Ephesians 3:19 tells us as we know the love of Christ, which surpasses knowledge, we will be filled up in the fullness of God. Ask Him to teach you about His love and show you what real love looks like and how it feels. He will faithfully visit you and reveal to you a love that is always constant and unconditional. He will lovingly share with you His love which never fails.

## Negative Beliefs

God only takes care of me when I am good.
People will love and accept me if I do nice things for them.
People will love me if I look beautiful or am popular.
I need people to approve of me so I am acceptable.
If I am not loved, I am not a worthy person.
If you upset people they will not like you.
I should value other's opinions over my own.
Be good all the time and don't cause any problems.
If I have money and am successful then I will be lovable.
God only loves me when I am patient and full of faith.

He loves me when I am good.
He doesn't love me when I am bad.

## Scriptural Truths

God is always looking out for my best interest; however He does
not always intervene in choices I may make.
Wearing a mask of performance to be accepted does not mean I
will be happy or content.
Placing value in material things over relationship will leave me
lonely and unhappy.
I am wonderfully made by God and my life is important to Him.
I am of eternal value to God.
God loves me.

## Scripture Meditations: "It is written..."

Deuteronomy 7:7-8a — "The Lord did not set His love on you,
nor chose you, because you were more in number than any of
the peoples, for you were the fewest of all peoples, but because
the Lord loved you and kept the oath which He swore to your
forefathers..."

Isaiah 51:16 — "I have put My words in your mouth, and have
covered you with the shadow of My hand, to establish the
heavens, to found the earth, and to say to Zion, 'You are My
people.'"

John 14:21b — "He that loves me will be loved of my Father, and I
will love him and disclose Myself to him."

Romans 5:8 — "But God demonstrates His own love toward us, in
that while we were yet sinners, Christ died for us."

Romans 8:32 — "He who did not spare His own Son, but delivered Him up for us all, how will He not also with Him freely give us all things?"

Romans 8:35,37 — "Who shall separate us from the love of Christ? Shall tribulation, or distress, or persecution, or famine, or nakedness, or peril, or sword? But in all these things we overwhelmingly conquer through Him who loved us."

Romans 8:38-39 — "For I am convinced that neither death, nor life, nor angels, nor principalities, nor things present, nor things to come, nor powers, nor height, nor depth, nor any other created thing, shall be able to separate us from the love of God, which is in Christ Jesus our Lord."

Ephesians 1:3-6 — "Blessed be the God and Father of our Lord Jesus Christ, who has blessed us with every spiritual blessing in the heavenly placed in Christ. Just as He chose us in Him, before the foundation of the world, that we should be holy and blameless before Him in love. He predestined us to adoption as sons through Jesus Christ to Himself, according to the kind intention of His will to the praise of the glory of His grace, which He freely bestowed on us in the Beloved."

John 13:34-35 — "A new commandment I give to you, that you love one another, even as I have loved you, that you also love one another. By this all men will know that you are My disciples, if you have love for one another."

1 Corinthians 13:4-7 — "Love is patient, love is kind, and is not jealous; love does not brag and is not arrogant, does not act unbecomingly; it does not seek its own, is not provoked, does not take into account a wrong suffered, does not rejoice in unrighteousness, but rejoices with the truth; bears all things, believes all things, hopes all things, endures all things."

# Reflections...

# 13
# THE BETRAYAL

Dishonesty and deception comes to mind when we think of betrayal. Experiencing unfaithfulness in any form can chip away at our trust and security, effecting family and relationships for a lifetime. In attempting to resolve the pain of betrayal and rejection, I have found there to be only one antidote that can bring complete healing to such loss and disillusionment; God's redeeming love.

My husband, Richard made contact with a ministry in Florida in 1987. The next year he announced it was time to consider moving to be with a community who specifically was studying God's covenants. Richard's desire was to hear God more clearly and if we could learn more about His covenants and how they apply to our lives, we would understand more about God and His character and develop a more intimate relationship with Him. I desired to develop a closer relationship with God, but I was not sure this was the way.

The thought of being plucked out of our lovely spiritual and physical community and leaving our jobs left me stunned, upset and fearful. *How would this affect our son? Who were these people?* I didn't want to leave! Trying to be supportive I packed our belongings, but inside I was becoming angry, resentful, fearful and depressed. I said good-bye to my lovely home, our church community, friends, our family, schools and jobs we all loved. We also said good-bye to our salaries and retirements. Upon arrival I was catapulted into culture shock. Exotic creatures greeted me on my door step as well as in my garage. Our rental sat right on a lagoon. I was screaming inside, "Ah!" It seemed that everywhere I went there were snakes, gators and lizards – oh my! It was hot and steamy. I missed the soft coolness of my native blue grass. God what are we doing here in

"Snakeland?"

Within weeks my greatest fear had come upon me. We had moved to be a part of a community we thought would bring life, but it had become dysfunctional and fruitless. Everything in my life was being affected. I had not only entered what appeared to be a cult-like community but I had also unknowingly entered the wilderness. During the next few years life was agony and nothing seemed to go untouched. No matter what I tried to do, nothing worked. My physical pain increased and what savings and retirement we had acquired was used to live on due to our meager salaries. The home we left behind had not sold, doubling our monthly house payments. Before we knew what hit us, poor investments coupled with mortgage debt led us into bankruptcy. Our son was trying to make the best of the situation, but it was evident he was unhappy listening to my ranting from anxiety and my arguments with Richard. My classroom was the size of a large closet with no air-conditioning, a musty mildewed carpet and furniture that looked like it had been saved from a fire. The pastor's wife would occasionally park in our driveway with a loaded gun, stating she was distressed and ready to take her life. I cried almost daily. *"Dear God, why did we move here?"* Fear tightened its grip each week as we experienced what seemed like continuous loss. It was similar to having a hook in your mouth and any way you turned, it hurt. Anger and resentment gripped my soul. I would try to get control of my life by criticizing, arguing, and making threats I was going to leave. But I didn't want to leave. I loved my husband and I loved and needed to protect my son. I wanted my family and life back.

My efforts in trying to hold my composure in front of our son failed. Caustic and angry remarks would exit my mouth and shoot like piercing arrows at my husband, landing on whoever was present. I felt like I was dying so I would fight to live. *Why were we here and how could God do this to us?* I would gird myself up to make it through my work day, returning home in tears and discouragement. I wanted to go home. This could not be God's will for us. There was no fruit in our lives, everything felt like death.

Our relationship was strained and my criticalness and resentment built a wall between us.

Richard still stood on his beliefs that we were to move to this forsaken place, but I just wanted to go home. *What happened to training and ministry? What happened to the white picket fence and the happy home?* We began to receive words that we had entered the desert. One sweet lady shared she saw me as a "rose in the desert." *What desert? I didn't want to be a rose in the desert! God doesn't place people in the desert! I don't believe that. Nobody said anything to me about being in a desert when I asked Jesus into my heart.*

## This Must Be the Desert

Life seemed unbearable. Some comfort was found in Scripture when I would read Deuteronomy 8:2, "And you shall remember all the way which the Lord your God has led you in the wilderness these forty years, that He might humble you, testing you, to know what was in your heart, whether you would keep His commandments or not." More revelation came as I read on with verse 3, "And He humbled you and let you be hungry, and fed you with manna which you did not know nor did your fathers know, that He might make you understand that man does not live by bread alone, but man lives by everything that proceeds out of the mouth of the Lord."

*Could these Scriptures really apply to me? Was God really trying to test me and humble me? Would He really do that?* As difficult as it was to believe, I slowly came to accept the fact I was out of control. This must be the desert, but I did not like it; and recognizing this process of developing dependence on God didn't make life any easier.

As my anger, grumbling, complaining and accusations continued, I unknowingly helped set the stage for my husband to search for comfort and encouragement elsewhere. He found it in the arms of a trusted friend. By 1991 he chose to confess to me his inappropriate relationship. I was stunned and totally destroyed.

My greatest fear had come upon me. That all too familiar sense of shock that takes you out of your body had returned. I couldn't breathe. I wanted to cry and scream at the same time. Anger pulsated through my mind and my body. *How could this happen? I thought he loved me?* I felt deceived and betrayed. I wanted to run away. There had to be somewhere I could be alone and feel safe. *What was I going to do?* I didn't want to tell my family or our son. *How could I handle this and keep our family together?*

The one thing in my life I had hoped for was a faithful husband, which had now been taken from me. *How could I ever trust him again? How could I ever trust anyone again? How could my friend deceive me and continue our relationship as if nothing had happened?* Every one of my life foundations had turned to sand. Discouragement and depression deepened. I didn't want to go out anymore or be around anyone. I did not trust anybody. The pain in my heart appeared like a fog in my head. *Who could I talk to? Who could I confide in?* I closed myself off from all relationships. I was like a robot getting up, going to work, coming home, doing household chores and going to church. *"I will try to get myself under control and forget about this,"* I thought to myself. *"Let's just try to get back to normal."* As I walked, I would look down and see my feet almost floating above the ground. *"I know you expect me to forgive Father, but how?"* I sensed nothing. I was once again detaching myself from life. I felt like the walking dead.

Whenever there is a breach in a relationship and communication ceases, a door is opened for infidelity and division. Richard wanted comfort and refuge from what he perceived as my harassment and control. I wanted a husband who would talk with me, share his thoughts with me, and allow me to have a voice in our decision-making. Now with revelation of his indiscretion, I just wanted him punished. I wanted the grief in my heart to go away. I wanted my life back. *"What am I going to do now God? Can You take this pain away?"*

## The Choice for Restoration

After days and weeks of prayer, I chose to remain with Richard, and I asked God to bring His counsel and truth into our relationship. We both made a commitment to try to heal our marriage. We knew we would need God's strength to help us forgive one another. I asked God to help me learn to love and trust my husband again. The relationship with my friend was also damaged and severed. Amazingly, I still loved and cared for her, but her betrayal left me disoriented and angry. *"Oh God, I am in deep pain. I can't feel my body or my emotions. I am overwhelmed with grief and despair. I can't forgive them right now God. Please don't leave me. I need You to help me forgive Father. This is too big for me. I can't see any hope. I can't do this alone."*

The next few years were extremely difficult. As I grieved the pain of this breach, anxiety and depression became my partners. They followed me to work everyday and back home. They were with me in the morning and when I tried to go to sleep. I sought counsel and threw myself into my work, hoping to find relief from the pain. My depression deepened. The doctor prescribed various medications for anxiety and depression, but it seemed like nothing could penetrate the darkness I sensed around me.

My brother came to visit in the summer of 1999. He is a psychologist and could see the signs that I could not see. He encouraged me to consider taking time off from work. I was crashing. It was inevitable. I had failed again. I soon resigned from my job. My work, my retirement and my life all came crumbling down and I spent the next year of my life in a deep dark abyss trying to figure out what went wrong and where was God in all of this.

The year, 2000, would be one of the darkest and loneliest years of my life, and yet God was still there beside me. He began to take me on an incredible journey of revelation to make sense of all my wounds, hurts and betrayals. His revelation and counsel came through books, tapes, messages, prophetic words and dreams that I began to experience. I had asked God to show me truth and He was answering my prayers. Little revelations would come concerning my perceptions of life. The study and work was challenging. My brain seemed foggy and it took energy each day to gain fresh perspective and truth. God began to breathe life back into my soul and spirit. He was connecting the dots to my trials and bringing healing and understanding to my soul (mind, will and emotions).

One night while in prayer, I sensed God saying that as I was healed on the inside, my outside or bodily healing would take place. I had no idea what this meant. It sounded so strange. *"Being healed on the inside would bring healing to my body?"* Through times of study I began to see how my emotions were affecting me. Scriptures became illuminated concerning forgiveness and repentance, which lead me to a deeper understanding of God's grace and mercy. I began to research who I was in Christ and see that God had made me acceptable, even when my natural circumstances were telling me I was not.

Day by day, revelation by revelation, my body began to respond. The pain began to diminish. I made a choice to forgive my husband and my friend; to trust God and to trust others again. I decided to choose to work at reconciliation. Hope was being breathed back into me. Each day I awoke with the desire to forgive. *"Lord, I choose to forgive today. Please help me forgive."* The anxiety and depression began to lift. The numbness in my body began to diminish and the colors in the earth looked vivid and bright again.

## Negative Beliefs

Fear of loss, of God's disapproval, man's disapproval.
Fear of not meeting cultural or worldly demands.
Fear of criticism from relatives, family and spiritual community.
Fear of not being able to make people happy.
Fear of not praying enough.
Fear of failure and not being productive.

You don't deserve good things happening to you.

It's his fault. It's my entire fault. It's God's fault.

When I am in control I feel secure and safe.

I will let others make choices for me so I can blame them if things don't work out.

Being right makes me feel secure.

God doesn't allow hard things to happen to His people.

## Scriptural Truths

If I do not deal with fear, it will eat up the life I have been given and it will overtake me.

Fear of not feeling I have done enough for God negates Jesus' crucifixion.

Blaming others only prolongs my denial and keeps me from the truth.

Believing I am in control of situations may set me up for a great fall.

My security is not in me or what I can achieve, but in God.

In life, I often cover my heart and try to be what others want me to be. Thus, I may not live life from my heart, where the springs of life flow.

## Scripture Meditations: "It is written..."

James 1:5 — "But if any of you lacks wisdom, let him ask of God, who gives to all men generously and without reproach, and it will be given to him."

3 John 1:2 — "Beloved, I wish above all things that you may prosper and be in good health, just as your soul prospers."

1 Thessalonians 5:23 — "Now may the God of peace Himself sanctify you entirely; and may your spirit and soul and body be

preserved complete, without blame at the coming of our Lord Jesus Christ."

Psalm 103:2-5 — "Bless the Lord, O my soul, and forget none of His benefits; Who pardons all your iniquities, Who heals all your diseases; Who redeems your life from the pit; Who crowns you with loving-kindness and compassion; Who satisfies your years with good things, so that your youth is renewed like the eagle.

Matthew 6:14-15 — "For if you forgive men for their transgressions, your heavenly Father will also forgive you. But if you do not forgive men, then your Father will not forgive your transgressions."

Acts 16:31 — "And they said, "Believe in the Lord Jesus, and you shall be saved, you and your household."

Romans 5:3-5 — "And not only this, but we also exult in our tribulations, knowing that tribulation brings about perseverance, and perseverance, proven character; and proven character, hope; and hope does not disappoint, because the love of God has been poured out within our hearts through the Holy Spirit who was given to us."

## Reflections...

# 14
# THE HEALING TEAM

Visitations of God appeared frequently during the mid 1990's with signs and wonders appearing in various congregations. Many in the Body rejoiced in the refreshing presence while others regarded the manifestations of laughing and crying, rolling and running with concern and doubt. It was a time of spiritual growth as well as a time of awakening, as I observed the schisms and underlying battles within the Church concerning what was considered from God, and what was not. What was considered holy and what was profane? It became more apparent that what we choose to focus on is what we make room for in our beliefs and in our lives.

Doors began to open to share the truths and healings I was experiencing in my own body by addressing my unscriptural thoughts and negative emotions. However, it would soon become apparent that some were skeptical to acknowledge the need for emotional healing in the Body of Christ.

I was asked to share my experience with a local healing team ministry. It appeared this community was curious to hear of the various ways God was working in my life. I was excited to present my experiences so others could be freed from the beliefs and strongholds keeping them from receiving God's blessings and life. The presentation was prepared, the night arrived and the truths were spoken. I hoped they would be encouraged by my story and would begin to understand why some people were not receiving immediate healing; but I was stunned by the silence that followed as I asked if there were any questions or discussion. The silence was painful. The bodies of the attendees moved in slow motion as they quietly exited the room. One dear lady came up to offer me a hug and a smile. The next gentleman simply laughed and said, "Man, *you've been quite a mess!"*

*Did I hear that correctly? It was easy to agree that I was a mess,
but had they heard the truth? Was that all this presentation was for, to
let me know what a big mess I was? Did I not share it correctly?* I felt
humiliated and discouraged. I shared my heart and what I believed
to be truth in my life and I was jokingly dismissed. Driving home
I felt grieved and saddened. Years later I would learn we make
room for what we focus on and in this case, this healing team
placed their emphasis on the importance of miracles and instant
healings. I love miracles and signs and wonders. God has touched
me many times with His miraculous intervention. However, I have
personally observed most healings have been a process and have
often required more than one intervention. The healings have
been progressive and have been coupled with counsel, revelation,
repentance, forgiveness and reconciliation. God is creative and
diverse. There are many ways He comes to bring His healing and
restoration.

It was also revelation to me the emotional challenges I
experienced may not be well received by many in the Church.
Nobody really wanted to discuss emotional or mental challenges.
I was supposed to be redeemed and already sanctified and if I
was experiencing mental conflict, it must be a demon or sin. I
began to work through the shame, embarrassment and sense of
rejection of being labeled a mess, emotionally ill, faithless, unsaved
or demonized. However, God continued to encourage me as He
comforted me through His word and the writings of others.

Receiving physical healing through emotional healing had not
been well received on that particular evening. However my quest for
understanding continued as I asked God for clarity and revelation.
Our Father desires to reveal to us the various ways He heals and
at times our healing may be connected to our mind and how we
think. God was illuminating unbiblical mindsets directing my life.
Through His healing touch, He had come to help me renew my
mind: "And do not be conformed to this word, but be transformed
by the renewing of your mind, that you may prove what the will of

God is, that which is good and acceptable and complete" (Romans 12:2).

## Negative Beliefs

I do not feel like what I have to share has value to others.

My spirituality is measured by how often I attend church or if they like what I say.

The more I attend church, the more the pastor and the community will like me.

I should only teach what the people in church want to hear.

Personal revelation is not relevant in the Body.

God expects me to always be strong and perfect.

## Scriptural Truths

My testimony is important in telling others about the many aspects of God.

I am to be conformed to God and His will, not to the desires of my family or friends.

Spirituality is based on a relationship with God and His word, not on what man may require from human doctrine.

It is more important to be acceptable to God than to man.

My value comes from God and not from man.

Religion can become a cover to hide emotional issues.

God desires to take me to a place of humility so I can address my weaknesses.

## Scripture Meditations: "It is written..."

Romans 12:1-2 — "I urge you therefore, brethren, by the mercies of God, to present your bodies a living and holy sacrifice, acceptable to God, which is your spiritual service of worship. And do not be conformed to this world, but be transformed by the renewing of your mind that you may prove what the will of God is, that which is good and acceptable and complete."

Psalm 34:19 — "Many are the afflictions of the righteous; but the Lord delivers him out of them all."

Galatians 3:13a — "Christ redeemed us from the curse of the Law, having become a curse for us."

Romans 8:38-39 — "For I am convinced that neither death, nor life, nor angels, nor principalities, nor things present, nor things to come, nor powers, nor height, nor depth, nor any other created thing, shall be able to separate us from the love of God, which is in Christ Jesus our Lord."

## Reflections...

_____

_____

_____

_____

_____

_____

_____

_____

_____

_____

_____

# 15
# THOUGHTS, EMOTIONS AND THE BODY

Medical science and research has been able to show our mind, emotions and body are intricately connected. There are various studies on the human brain which describe the complex connection between the thought pathways of the brain and our body's hormonal system, which secretes the chemicals that signal our brain and organs to function properly. When we respond to our environment with negative thoughts such as fear or anger, our glandular system shoots out hormones like cortisol or adrenaline to assist our body in dealing with the stress. When a person experiences long periods of stress that go unresolved, the imbalance of these chemicals and hormones being released continually throughout our bodies, can begin to have an adverse effect.

In her book, *Who Switched Off My Brain?* Dr. Caroline Leaf has compiled extensive research regarding the intricacies of the brain. She shares insights and discoveries from several studies including Dr. Candace Pert, a neuroscientist and author[13] whose compelling findings suggest a biomolecular basis for our emotions. Dr. Pert's study reveals this important link between the mind and the body. Also presented is the work of another pioneering researcher, Dr. Marion Diamond, whose research links the thought life and emotions with the body. Dr. Diamond's findings basically suggest the evidence of chemicals, connected to our emotions and thought life, which are carried through the bloodstream, enabling "information molecules" to cause change at the cellular level affecting the body's cells and DNA.[14] From her research, Dr. Caroline Leaf concludes that approximately "eighty-seven percent of illnesses can be attributed to our thought life, and approximately thirteen percent to diet, genetics and environment. Other studies conclusively link certain chronic diseases, also known as lifestyle diseases, to an epidemic of toxic emotions in our culture."[15]

Dr. Leaf suggests that a sudden burst of stress will lower our immunity. What she terms as toxic waste is caused by our toxic thoughts and emotions coupled with extreme stress. Dr. Leaf asserts that toxic waste may both weaken our immune system and contribute to certain health issues which may include: Type 1 diabetes, cancer, asthma, allergies, eczema and skin problems, migraines, Crohn's diseases, hypertension, strokes, angina, arthritis, lupus, fybromyaligia, constipation, diarrhea, nausea, vomiting, ulcers, irritable bowel syndrome, fertility problems, muscle tension in the neck, back and throat, infections, colds, depression, phobias, fatigue, insomnia, anxiety, poor memory, lack of creativity, panic attacks and more.[16] She further states that Dr. John Sorno, a professor of clinical rehabilitation medicine at the New York University School of Medicine theorizes that most back pain may result from psychological issues. His book, *The Divided Mind: The Epidemic of Mindbody Disorders* [17], discusses what is termed psychosomatic disorders. According to Dr. Sorno, an illness is labeled psychosomatic when doctors are not able to find any physical cause, and thus, they often dismiss the symptoms as being "just in your mind." Dr. Leaf states: "While their diagnosis is right, their reasoning is wrong. Thoughts do cause illness and should thus be studied and controlled. If they are powerful enough to make us sick, they are powerful enough to make us healthy as well."[18]

What tender direction and guidance God reveals when we read His words in Philippians 4:8 to think on "whatever is true, whatever is honorable, whatever is right, whatever is pure, whatever is lovely, whatever is of good character, if there is any excellence and if anything worthy of praise, let your mind dwell on these things." God's instructions and statutes were never meant to be demanding or legalistic, but to guide us toward life, health and prosperous living. Just as the Apostle Paul encouraged the church at Corinth to take every thought captive so they would prosper and not be destroyed: "Casting down imaginations, and every high thing that exalts itself against the knowledge of God, and bringing into captivity every thought to the obedience of Christ" (2 Corinthians 10:5).

Scripture teaches in 1 Thessalonians 5:23 we are formed with a body, soul and spirit: "Now may the God of peace Himself, sanctify you entirely; and may your spirit and soul and body be preserved complete." Drawing from the research of scientists and specialists such as Dr. Leaf, we begin to understand that we are an amazing and complex creation interacting with nature, other human beings and with God. Without the peace of God to "preserve us complete" as stated above, our complexity can lead to unbalanced responses. For example, sometimes traumas are so painful we are unable to assimilate our experience in a healthy manner. We may become overwhelmed with stress, rejection, loss, loneliness, disappointments and heartache, poor decisions, verbal or physical abuse. In some cases, such as grief from loss, major life changes, or even life transitions, it is natural and even healthy to experience emotional pain. However, as suggested by Dr. Leaf, if we fail to resolve these emotions over a reasonable period of time, we may begin to experience symptoms of a physical nature.

We are told in Psalm 103:3 that God forgives us of all our iniquities and He heals us of all our diseases. During my illness, I would meditate daily on Isaiah 53:4-6: "He was wounded for our transgressions, he was bruised for our iniquities: the chastisement of our peace was upon him; and with his stripes we are healed." But I was still battling physical pain and other illness without relief. When I began to reflect on 3 John 1:2, a light began to open up in my mind that maybe my soul was diseased: "Beloved, I wish above all things that thou may prosper and be in health, even as your soul prospers." God wanted my soul to prosper! I began to pray about my soul and my illnesses. I reflected on the peaceful quiet voice within me that once said, *When you are healed inside, the outside manifestation of your healing will take place.* I could only respond with a prayer: "Oh God, *help me to understand what You are saying. Show me Your truth and what is inside of me that might hinder the healing touch of Your hand."*

In the 1980's, as I battled chronic, debilitating pain, my physician, not finding any physical reason for my pain, looked at me and declared, *"You're fine, it's all in your head."* Many years later, I have come to understand that his diagnosis proved to be basically correct, but at that moment, the pain was real and my undiagnosed anxiety and depression continued to support the physical symptoms I was experiencing. When another wise physician encouraged me to journal events that occurred 24 to 48 hours before I experienced increased muscle spasms and pain, I began to see a correlation between my emotional response to events and my physical pain. Maybe this was true. Maybe, just maybe, the years of pain coupled with various other illnesses in my life, were somehow connected to my brain and how I had emotionally responded to situations in my life.

With this revelation I continued my journey, reading books and receiving counsel as I searched to understand my thoughts and my responses to life. I began to see how even submersing myself into my spiritual faith could not free me from the unscriptural beliefs I had developed over time. I finally acknowledged that I could not find any silver bullet or prayer that was going to quickly release me from the anxiety and depression. It was now evident I would be embarking upon an arduous and painful path of unwinding the unhealthy thought processes of my mind and developing healthy and scriptural patterns of thinking.

In my efforts to align my thought patterns and beliefs with God's Word, I continued to gain insight through books, counsel and prayer. Journaling allowed me to review and meditate on my daily experience, thoughts and responses to life. I found many of my misperceptions resulted from three primary negative thoughts, as suggested by Dr. Albert Ellis and Dr. Aaron Beck. They are: 1) I must do well, 2) You must treat me well, and 3) The world must be easy.[19] It made sense to me that I was not living in reality by thinking in this manner. Obviously, none of us do well all the time. Certainly, everyone is mistreated at sometime in their life. We all make poor choices, and bad things do happen to good people, therefore, life is not always easy or fair. From here I began to develop my own list of thoughts which went beyond the three mentioned by Dr. Ellis. I sought to replace those thoughts with Scriptures and Biblical truths which God has provided. You may recognize some of these beliefs in your own life. Or you may find it worthwhile to ask God to help you discover other unhealthy beliefs that may be separating you from being preserved complete as God intends.

## Negative Beliefs

I am not acceptable if I make a poor choice.
I must be right.
I can't talk with anyone or let them know how I really feel.
No one can understand how I feel.
If I just don't think about it, I will feel better.
I need the world to be easy for me.
If I'm sick then I will receive love.
If I'm sick they will leave me alone.

## Scriptural Truths

I am unconditionally loved by God. I do not need to be sick to feel safe.
If I choose to focus on good things in my life, I will be more at peace.
I receive life and health when I attend to God's word.
Physical healing often begins from the inside (thoughts and emotions), bringing healing to the outside (physical body).
It is good to expect a miracle, but healing often includes the process of renewing my mind, will and emotions.
It is good to listen to my body. It is communicating how I am

feeling and what I am thinking.

## Scripture Meditations: "It is written..."

1 Thessalonians 5:23 — "Now may the God of peace Himself sanctify you entirely; and may your spirit and soul and body be preserved complete."

Philippians 4:8 — "Whatever is true, whatever is honorable, whatever is right, whatever is pure, whatever is lovely, whatever is of good character, if there is any excellence and if anything worthy of praise, let your mind dwell on these things."

2 Corinthians 10:5 — "We are destroying speculations and every lofty thing raised up against the knowledge of God, and we are taking every thought captive to the obedience of Christ."

1 John 2:1-2 — "I am writing these things to you that you may not sin (miss the mark). And if anyone sins, we have an Advocate with the Father, Jesus Christ, the righteous; and He Himself is the atonement for our sins; and not for ours only, but also for the whole world."

Proverbs 4:20-23 — "Listen, son of mine, to what I say. Listen carefully. Keep these thoughts ever in mind; let them penetrate deep within your heart, for they will mean real life for you, and radiant health. Above all else, guard your affections. For they influence everything else in your life" (Living Bible).

## Reflections...

# 16
# ARE OUR BELIEFS OUR DECEPTIONS?

I f someone were to ask me, *"What is one of the greatest deceptions for the Church today?"* I would have to respond with one word – Strongholds. In my own life and those we have served and counseled for the last thirty years, we have continually observed the deceptions of strongholds or unbiblical beliefs that have led to broken marriages and relationships, family and church division, job loss, financial loss, even political and government divisions. Often the cries for God to move appear to be unanswered, when our beliefs and choices are really what stand in the way of our obtaining the abundant life.

In Second Corinthians Paul wrote a letter to the church warning and correcting them against legalism and instructing them in their duty as Christians. The overall message was that they needed to be loyal to Christ and not to human personalities. He encouraged them to not look at things according to the outward appearance but by the Spirit and the Word.

Paul states: "For though we walk in the flesh, we do not war after the flesh; for the weapons of our warfare are not of the flesh, but divinely powerful in God for pulling down strongholds. We are destroying speculation and every high thing that exalts itself against the knowledge of God and we are taking every thought captive to the obedience of Christ" (2 Corinthians 10:3-5). Our weapons come from God. They help us to destroy strongholds which are unbiblical beliefs or fortresses in our thoughts that hinder us from the blessings of being His child.

## Paradigms, Attitudes, Perceptions, Strongholds

When we come to Christ we are changed and made new in

Him as Scripture states in 2 Corinthians 5:17: "Therefore if any man be in Christ, he is a new creature: old things are passed away; behold all things become new." But, we bring our old patterns of thinking or our earthly nature with us. All of our memories and experiences we have processed over a lifetime still remain in our mind. They do not automatically vanish from our thoughts when we accept Christ. There are many incorrect beliefs that are shrouded in piety or religious tradition. They may remain filed away in our brain waiting to be pulled out at a moment's notice. Our learned behaviors and beliefs help us to respond to daily activities and stimuli we encounter. Some of our beliefs are positive, but others may be lethal. If not dealt with, these old mind sets can control our lives and cause much pain and loss.

There is often an impression among Christians that after we receive Christ we will sail through life without challenges or difficulties. Reality, as well as Scripture, shows us this is far from the truth. Throughout God's Word we are encouraged to fight the good fight, labor, press on and persevere. We are born again (1 Peter 1:3); we are a new creation (2 Corinthians 5:17); we are accepted (Romans 15:7); we are secure (Romans 8:38-39); we are blessed with every spiritual blessing (Ephesians 1:3); and we are not condemned (Romans 8:1). However, John 13:14-17 instructs we are now disciples, and disciples learn to become like their teacher, which signifies change. Our Christian life is a process and is often hard work.

After salvation we are presented with the process of transformation and the job of submitting to the work of Holy Spirit, who patiently transforms us into Christ's character and likeness. Our sins have been forgiven and we are now seated with Christ; but many of our learned belief systems from the world, family, government, schools or churches will now begin to be revealed to us, so we can give them to Christ at the Cross and have Him put them to death.

So, what is a stronghold? It is a belief system or structure, a fortress, or our attitude and perception about life. There are unbiblical strongholds or belief systems that keep us from receiving God's promises, His freedom and His life. There are personal strongholds, emotional strongholds, worldview strongholds, religious strongholds and strongholds of past sins. They are attitudes, desires and responses from our old former life before accepting Christ. They are usually things that are not good for us or which may harm us. They do not line up with God's biblical principles or His universal laws.

When we ask God to reveal strongholds within us, He will often use life experiences to reveal the issue or unbiblical thought pattern. Traditions are often strongholds in families. *"In my family we have always done it this way."* Such a belief can easily develop into control, by not allowing a person to make different choices or be free. I have seen children in families have difficulty moving into new jobs or destiny, simply because their belief system told them they should never leave where they grew up. Or, a person may say *"I don't need anyone to help me."* In believing this, they may close themselves off from God, family, friends or community and miss the covenant blessing.

Horoscopes or secret societies can also bind us to beliefs or actions we accept as truth; just as the belief that if we break a superstition we will be hurt or experience calamity. *"You are a failure; you will never amount to anything. You are a black sheep."* Things we hear, things spoken over us, or our experiences often become our beliefs and can cause us to make harmful choices.

Ask God to reveal patterns of thinking in your life which may not line up with His Word, His nature or His character. He loves you and wants to see you succeed. He loves to reveal His truths to those who will ask and seek Him. "Ask, and it shall be given to you; seek, and you shall find; knock, and it shall be opened to you. For everyone who asks receives, and he who seeks finds, and to him who knocks it shall be opened" (Matthew 7:7).

# The Story of Little Girl

Once upon a time there was a precious little girl. Her smile would make the room glow. She was happy just to feel the breeze in her hair and look up at the sun and feel its warmth shining down from the azure sky. It made her feel warm and peaceful. She loved to run through the corn rows of her grandpa's farm and sneak down to the barn alone where she would quietly walk in and touch the soft fuzzy noses of the cows eating their supper. There she found such peace and quiet. The large brown eyes of the cattle seemed to speak to her. They were gentle and welcoming as they calmly gazed at her. They seemed to enjoy her visits.

She would look forward to spring when the beautiful long row of flowers planted by her grandpa would pop up from the once frozen ground. They would greet her and smile brightly with their glorious colors and petals pointing toward heaven. They made her feel happy inside. And oh, how she enjoyed jumping into the swing on the hill overlooking the street and the church just down the road as the leaves waved gently above her in the large maple tree. Its branches hung over her like a beautiful canopy of protection and happiness as she swung to and fro. Life was so precious and full of joy.

When grandmother would call everyone in for supper she would excitedly sit at the table waiting on her turn to savor the mashed potatoes and gravy and the fresh green beans from the garden. Dinnertimes were a family time of fun and conversation. The delicious food would re-energize her for play throughout the rest of each day.

After summer she returned to school. Her father was a principal of a large high school. She was very proud of him and how hard he worked. He provided a nice home, clothes and travel for her and her family. He had to be at work many hours, day and night, managing the school activities and education of the many students he cared for. He would bring presents back from his visits and school trips. Little Girl loved her father very much. Her father periodically would tell Little Girl how important it was for her and her brothers to be good and well-behaved, so they would be accepted and liked in the community. It was important to Little Girl to make her father proud.

At school Little Girl worked very hard to be loved and accepted. She would try out to be a cheerleader, but she was too tall and not cute enough. She would try out for plays, but she was not dramatic or very talented. She worked hard at her studies, trying to be smart enough, but she was unable to make good grades like her brothers. Fortunately, Little Girl had a few close friends, but there were others who would make fun of her and laugh at her clothes. They would call her names and make jokes about how she looked. She was asked to some parties, but mostly she was alone, working each day to be smart, beautiful and lovable.

Little Girl's mother was also a very hard worker. She made beautiful clothes and delicious meals for the family. She was always busy making sure the house was clean and that everyone was happy. The fragrance of her homemade cinnamon rolls were a special treat and made Little Girl and her brothers smile as they returned from school. She worked tirelessly to watch over her family. She encouraged the children to work hard and to stay nice and clean. Little Girl loved her mother very much and wanted her mother to be very proud of her too.

As she began to grow Little Girl began to take on many chores for the family. She scrubbed and waxed the floors, ironed the clothes and dusted the house. She cleaned off the table and washed the dishes nightly. She would volunteer to mow the grass and cut the shrubs, helping wherever needed. The more she accomplished, the more she hoped she would be noticed and loved.

Now she had two brothers who were very important to her family. As they grew they practiced night and day to become great athletes that would make their father and mother very proud. During sports season the family would go every Friday to the sports complex to watch their sons play. The brothers would play very well and score many points. The parents would sometimes get upset if their sons did not play a perfect game or play as well as they could. This saddened Little Girl because she was most proud of their talents and achievements. The little girl was happy going to the game and eating popcorn and sitting with her friends. She was very proud of how hard her brothers played and how successful they appeared. She loved to cheer for them. After the weekend games they would all go home and Little Girl would return to cleaning the house, mowing the lawn, trimming the scrubs, washing and waxing the wood floors and cleaning the dishes.

One day Little Girl decided to sing in the choir. She loved to sing. Singing made her feel happy inside. She would sing and sense herself exploding with joy. Singing lifted her into the heavens. When she sang the sky seemed bluer and the sun was brighter. The colors of the world would shout at her with excitement. She sang and sang for many years all by herself. She would sing with records and sing in her room and in the garage. She would sing at camp and sing in her music class. One day she was asked to go to a competition to sing. She asked permission to go. She had so much fun at the competition singing along with her friends. At the end of the competition she was awarded four gold medals for Class A singing. Nobody was able to see her sing but she took her medals home to show her family. Her parents said, *"That's nice,"* and continued with their work. They were occupied with making a living, trying hard to provide for the family and placing food on the table. They would discuss the boys and their sports, how many points they made and how many games they would win as well as where they would get scholarships and where they would go to school. They would discuss the newspaper clippings and how everyone was talking about how great they were at sports. She put the medals away and every so often would take them out to see how pretty they were and to remember how much fun she had and what she had accomplished.

As Little Girl grew older, she began to sing in a larger ensemble at the university. She not only sang, but she was able to dance. She and her friends performed wonderful music numbers and large crowds would come to hear the beautiful songs that were sung. She enjoyed herself with her friends knowing her family was very busy and had little time to come see her perform. But, it wasn't enough.

Before long, Little Girl was asked to perform in a pageant. She was asked to sing as her talent. If she won she would also get scholarship money and maybe get her name in the paper. She drove herself to the pageant, her family was very busy and it would be difficult to attend. She was excited to try to compete with other girls and see if she was considered beautiful enough and talented enough to be favored above the rest. She worked very hard and sang her best. The final girls were announced. Little Girl was called to be a finalist in the pageant. She cried. It was overwhelming that at last, she might be seen as special enough to win. Maybe people would really like her and think she was special. Maybe her mother and father and brothers would talk about how skilled she was or how beautiful she was. Maybe she would become successful and more people would love and approve of her.

The final night of the pageant came. She had been judged in swimsuit and evening gown. Now it was time for her talent. The curtain was rising. *"Oh God, if it is not Your will don't let me win,"* she said. Little Girl did her best and waited on the judges to share their results. They called her name with two other little girls. There were three contestants left on stage. They called her name next. Little Girl was only the second runner-up. She did not win the contest. She did not show that she was the best or most beautiful. She was disappointed. *"Oh well,"* she thought, *"I had a wonderful time and it was fun, but I do not think I will do this again. There will be something new tomorrow."*

She went home with her trophies. She was so glad to be home. As she entered the door her family was there to greet her. She was hoping they would be happy at what she had achieved for them. She hoped that she would hear them say, *"Congratulations, we are so proud of you."* As she entered the door, they smiled and said *"Good job!"* But at that moment she also heard someone declare, *"You didn't really want to win. You could have won!"* Little Girl's heart sank. It wasn't enough. She had not been good enough. She put on her happy face as she often did, gave a little laugh and said, *"I tried my best."* But in her heart she knew that her best had not been good enough, and that she would need to try harder to be better and more successful to have her family love her more and tell her how proud they were of her. She would look for things in her future that would help her prove that she was good enough and that she deserved to be loved.

Little Girl went back to work attending school, mowing the grass, trimming the shrubs, sweeping and waxing the floors, cleaning up the dishes and ironing the clothes, not knowing that she was already loved and valued. She had developed a paradigm or belief system that became a stronghold in her life. She thought she was not valuable or successful enough to receive love. She would need to work harder and perform greater feats to be considered important enough to be loved and accepted. She would have to be happier, prettier, more humorous, brighter, and more accomplished in her job. She would have to strive to find new ways to be acceptable and admired. She would have to work harder and perform better. She would need to work for awards that would validate her existence; then, people would think she was special and love her.

So Little Girl continued to find ways to prove that she was valuable and acceptable to live in this world. She became a homecoming queen. She must be acceptable if she won the votes of her university classmates. She was able to rest and feel assured for a short time. Then it was back to work. She began to daily look for situations where she could help others and also feel good about who she was. She chose to work in Education where she could help children. How she loved the children. So each day in her job, she chose to work very hard. Working harder and longer would help her do great things for the children while giving her some contentment. After many years, Little Girl was recognized as a valuable teacher and she won Teacher of the Year Awards. As much as she loved the children and she appreciated the awards,

Little Girl could never find the key to fill the hole in her heart. She continued to search and search for the missing piece of the puzzle where she could at last find peace and contentment.

## A Key to Success

Just like Little Girl, experiences in our lives can cause us to develop hidden desires and motivations. Our perceptions and responses to life help develop our belief systems. These beliefs are our foundation on how we live life. We all want to be loved, cared for and acknowledged as valuable. We desire to have peace in our lives and a sense that we have a fulfilling purpose on this earth. Fear of man or the need to please man develops early in a child's life. We may perceive success in life as being accepted by men and the world's principles, instead of recognizing that true success comes when we begin to love and value ourselves. Spiritual success comes when we understand the importance of having a relationship with a loving and wise Father, who encourages us to walk in His statutes as He guides us on the path to joy and peace.

Sometimes our life experiences do not coincide with our hopes or desires. We may begin to view failure or rejection as a barometer showing us that we are not good enough or smart enough. We may feel that we are not lovable or valued and we will never succeed or feel satisfied. Our thoughts begin to develop into certain beliefs or paradigms, which then lay the foundation for our future choices, decisions and ultimately our happiness and contentment or loss and pain.

In looking at Little Girl's life experience, she inwardly wanted to be loved and be looked upon by her parents, her family and society as being valuable. Her need for man's approval as well as her fear of man, of criticism or judgment, propelled her toward incorrect perceptions of her life as well as continual disappointments. Even though her parents loved her dearly, she perceived the need to always do more. Each achievement or success only brought another rung on the ladder to climb, and she struggled to attain an unreachable goal. She believed if her parents were proud of her, then she would feel valuable, loved, and accepted. And if she could just attain that elusive achievement she could finally be happy and whole.

In all the different ways she tried to perform to get the love she desired she always appeared to fail. Each achievement brought a sense that it was just never enough. After years of not accomplishing or fulfilling her needs Little Girl began to experience disappointment, and a belief that she would never attain her goal to be lovable and good enough. She developed a paradigm telling her *"she would never be loved or valued so she could feel peace and completeness."* Her parents were very good to her and provided food, a nice home and clothing, even a car and their human love. She had everything she could ever need or want, except contentment in her heart. Her parents sacrificed and worked very hard to see that she could have a happy successful life. They tried to show her that she was really loved. But she still felt alone, rejected, unhappy and angry with herself and her life. She had developed a need for approval that was costly. Her need for success coupled with a lack of hope chiseled away at any confidence she would ever attain greatness. She began to realize she would never be able to do enough to be accepted and loved, which caused her to develop depression and anxiety. She also began to develop other fears and phobias. She became obsessive and compulsive in many of her daily activities, trying to be perfect and in control of her life. Negative thoughts and beliefs began to form in her mind. She entertained fear and anxiety daily, afraid she would never find peace and acceptance.

In Little Girl's search for significance she tried to control things in her life. The more control she exerted the more her life seemed to spiral out of control. In her journey, she came to understand there are two paths to choose in life. The first path she chose was a life centered on her self and her own desires. She focused on trying very hard to meet her own personal needs. Basically, her response to life, often subconsciously, flowed from her thoughts of *"How is this going to affect me and my life?"* Would her needs and expectations be met? Would she receive significance or reward? Even though she searched for love, self-acceptance, significance and wholeness she felt empty and unfulfilled.

On her second path, much later in her life, Little Girl found love, acceptance and significance. She found a path that began to heal the hole in her heart that she was never able to fill. On this path she began to find peace, acceptance and the security she had always longed for. She found her life in choosing to live for God.

However, even in her choice to serve God, it was necessary for her to understand the human drive in her: the need for significance. In religion, she had perceived her good works would give her life and fill the empty void in her spirit, and her obsessive behaviors and rituals would be acceptable. As we choose to live for God, we must understand that our unmet needs or desires can become works in the name of the Lord. In this deception we may exalt ourselves and try to find new venues for the same old need for approval and significance. We just begin to do great works in God's name instead of our own.

Submitting to God allows Him to reveal our hidden motivations, by Holy Spirit dividing our soul from our spirit, which helps us to learn to move out in the things of God instead of our own purposes and vain imaginations. Developing an intimate relationship and learning to hear the Spirit of God will bring true guidance, wholeness and security as we learn to lay down our control and allow Him to direct our lives.

When we as children have difficulty processing experiences, whether in our families, schools or personal relationships, we develop belief systems which help support us as we try to make sense of life so we can live well in this world. We as human beings are all on a search for significance and wholeness. We all have also experienced traumas and hurts, wounding or rejection at one time or another. How did we respond to these experiences? How did we process them? Did we respond or react with healthy beliefs? Was our reaction "all about me?", or were we able to see a bigger picture? Did we react out of an ungodly belief or stronghold?

# Strongholds Affect Everyone

When we develop a stronghold, we have developed an unbiblical belief system or structure. It is called a stronghold because it becomes ingrained in our reasoning and our thoughts. We begin to view our experiences and life through that stronghold. It begins to hinder us from receiving the promises and blessings of God. We may begin to make poor choices or live in regret. It keeps us from God's freedom and His resurrection life.

There are many different kinds of unbiblical beliefs or structures we may develop. These strongholds may be found in our past sin. Please remember when we talk of sin, it is nothing more than "missing the mark," which we all experience at one time or another in our lives. In his book, *Demolishing Strongholds*, David Devenish brings light to the various areas where strongholds may develop including: occult activity, spiritualism like séances, mediums and horoscopes, magic, Satanism, New Age, superstition, religious legalism which scripture describes as a "doctrine of demons" (1 Timothy 4:1-5), Freemasonry, sexual activities including distortion of role models, pornography and soul ties. He also identifies strongholds found in our culture, government, families and emotions as well.[20]

Religious strongholds or unbiblical beliefs can be found in the local church as well as in denominations, usually developing from weak biblical foundations. Bitterness, rebellion, division, leadership that dominates or manipulates, humanistic teaching and sexual immorality are just a few.

There are cultural strongholds like atheism, hedonism or the pursuit of pleasure, individualism or "me first", the love of mammon which aligns itself with greed and lust, and world views which are developed through our training in our educational system that affects the way we think. You may have heard the phrase, *"Eat, drink and be merry, for tomorrow we may die."* This is considered a Post Modernism stronghold which is obviously illogical and unbiblical in thought, but there are many who have chosen to live by this belief.

Governmental strongholds are very apparent, particularly in election years. Scripture basically teaches two concepts in political government: 1) those in authority have been placed there by God and 2) we are to submit ourselves to the rule of paying taxes. Strongholds or unbiblical structures may develop in countries through dictatorships, genocide, homosexuality and abortion.

Family strongholds can be observed in unhealthy family "traditions," when we say, *"We've just always done it this way in our family."* Or, *"We always have Christmas Eve at our house."* Being controlled or enabled by a family member can make it difficult for a child to grow up, marry and live their life successfully.

Emotional strongholds of rejection, indecisiveness, irresponsibility, negativity, passivity, rejection, being fatalistic or resentful, holding bitterness or un-forgiveness can be birthed in misunderstandings and poor communication, as well as in premeditated hurtful actions.

What we think and perceive about life is important for living well. I found paradigms and unscriptural beliefs held me back from joy, peace and health for a great deal of my life. Let's continue to explore together some of the ways we may have responded to our life experiences, traumas and hurts which may have taken place in our families, schools, home, work and in our church community. Sometimes our responses can create separation or division in our lives. We may choose to isolate ourselves or build a wall of protection so we will not have to experience any further pain. When we choose to begin to look at beliefs that may have gained a foothold in our lives, we can then embark upon a journey toward freedom, blessing, healing, restoration and peace.

Maybe you have become aware of an unhealthy paradigm in your life you would like to address. I have found this prayer to help me begin the journey.

---

*"Father, I am asking You to search my heart and reveal in me any hindrance that has kept me from receiving Your love,*

*Your life, and Your blessings. Please reveal situations, responses, beliefs, or judgments I have made and believed that do not line up with Your truth. Bring revelation to me and help me to see the lies and falsehoods I have believed. I invite You to help me and give You permission, Lord, to renew my mind with Your truth and revelation. Thank you for Your love and faithfulness and for shining Your light on the dark things in my heart."*

## Negative Beliefs

I will never be successful.

I am unlovable.

Every time I try something, it fails.

No matter what I do it is never right.

It is never enough.

I don't know how to be successful.

If I just achieve this, then I will be happy.

## Scriptural Truths

God gives me the strength and wisdom to succeed.

God gives me the ability to make wealth.

In my weakness, God is able to reveal His strength and provision.

True peace comes when I am content in God's provision.

When I learn to love myself, I can begin to love others.

God will expose beliefs and attitudes in me so I can live a more abundant life.

## Scripture Meditations: "It is written..."

Ephesians 4:22-24 — "...in reference to your former manner of life, you lay aside the old self, which is being corrupted in accordance with the lusts of deceit, and that you be renewed in the spirit of your mind, and put on the new self, which in the likeness of God has been created in righteousness and holiness of the truth."

2 Corinthians 5:17 — "Therefore if any man be in Christ, he is a new creature: old things are passed away; behold, all things are become new."

Romans 1:21 — "For even though they knew God, they did not honor Him as God, or give thanks; but they became futile in their speculations, and their foolish heart was darkened."

Matthew 6:33 — "Seek first the kingdom of God, and his righteousness; and all these things will be added unto you."

Philippians 4:6-7 — "Be anxious for nothing but in everything by prayer and supplication with thanksgiving let your requests be made known to God. And the peace of God which surpasses all comprehension, shall guard your hearts and your minds in Christ Jesus."

Philippians 4:19 — "And my God shall supply all your needs according to His riches in glory in Christ Jesus."

Philippians 1:21 — "For to me, to live is Christ and to die is gain."

Ephesians 2:10 — "For we are His workmanship, created in Christ Jesus for good works, which God prepared beforehand, that we should walk in them."

Romans 5:8 — "But God demonstrates His own love toward us, in that while we were yet sinners, Christ died for us."

Romans 8:35,37-39 — "Who shall separate us from the love of Christ? Shall tribulation, or distress, or persecution, or famine, or nakedness, or peril, or sword? But in all these things we overwhelmingly conquer through Him who loved us. For I am convinced that neither death, nor life, nor angels, nor principalities, nor things present, nor things to come, nor power, nor height, nor depth, nor any other created things, shall be able to separae us from the love of God, which is in Christ Jesus our Lord."

## Reflections...

# 17
# PERFORMANCE AND
# HIDDEN MOTIVATIONS

We develop performance from the time we are born. Mama and Daddy lean over the crib and laugh with glee as we babble and begin to form sounds. When we begin potty training we are met with a "good girl" or "good boy" as we achieve success and do our business in the potty. There is no way around learning to perform or to respond to applause. Everyone develops different levels and responses to performing and there is not one parent who will be able to watch over a child without in some way encouraging their desire to be loved and accepted. Nor will any parent be able to protect their child from feeling the sense of rejection or failure.

The need to perform develops in many ways and its tentacles are found hidden in almost everything we do. Life becomes a product to be packaged and developed instead of a gift to enjoy and savor. Our thoughts focus on the process of how to achieve acceptance, favor and success. We can become consumed with the need to exalt ourselves which causes us to veer off the path of who we were really meant to be.

When we have been rejected or have been exposed to negative physical or verbal experiences, performance or perfectionism may develop. Being able to perform is not evil in itself. But if the need for approval, to be recognized or validated begins to appear obsessive and to control one's decisions and life, then a stronghold may be present that places the person in a vicious cycle of never achieving enough or having enough. Excessive work habits and choices can spiral one into a life out of balance where sickness and disease are waiting to gain hold.

# The Mind's Deceptions

Sometimes our mind fools us into believing we are doing a good work or someone is in need of our services. We can become an overachiever or a workaholic for what appears to be very good reason. Only when we search the motivations of our heart can we begin to understand if our quest is righteous or if it is simply birthed from our need for validation and love.

Dr. Larry Crabb shares in his book *Effective Biblical Counseling* that guilt, anxiety and resentment are three problem emotions we were not designed to carry. He states that in not addressing the assumptions that helped us develop these emotions; we will find either a temporarily satisfying goal or eventually reach some form of breakdown. In our drive to obtain security or safety we can develop phobias, sexual dysfunction, obsessive-compulsive behaviors and other neurosis.

In his illustration, Dr. Crabb tells the story of a person who developed a fear of crossing bridges. The person had to cross a major bridge everyday to get to his work. The client had no difficulty crossing the bridge until he was given a promotion at work. He then began to develop fear and anxiety. Further analysis revealed to Dr. Crabb that his client's self-worth was being threatened and that the root issue was his fear of failure. The man desired the significance and success related to his new job, but the fear of failure hindered him from enjoying the advancement. The client could have chosen to acknowledge his fear and receive counsel and support to overcome this obstacle and accept his new position; but he subconsciously chose to attach his fear to the bridge he crossed everyday by developing and maintaining a fear of bridges. In reality, Dr. Crabb's client chose to relinquish a well earned new position to a crippling fear of failure. He quit his job and took a safe position in a firm on the other side of the bridge.[21]

Earlier we learned how our emotions can manifest in sickness or disease. We can also now see from Dr. Crabb's illustration that our belief systems can affect our life choices and decision making.

When we choose not to take responsibility for our thoughts or emotions we may find ourselves in devastating circumstances wondering what went wrong or blaming our problems on God. It is important to examine ourselves and search for any hidden beliefs or motivations that can hinder us from experiencing a healthy and joyful life. Having a relationship with God does not make us exempt from emotional or physical challenges; it simply gives us the hope of healing, comfort, restoration, redemption, divine guidance, provision, counsel and eternal life.

All human beings have basic needs such as: *Physical* - food, water and shelter to maintain life; *Security* - knowing that our basic needs are met; *Love* - having a sense of acceptance and belonging; and *Significance* - sensing who we are and that we are of value. Hidden motivations and our need to attain basic needs can drive us to unrealistic expectations; just as fear, anxiety, guilt, resentment or un-forgiveness can color our perceptions of life and hinder us from living a full and rewarding life. The unresolved fear of death can also quietly hide in our thoughts and propel us onto a path of panic and despair and ultimately devastating choices.

What a magnificent covenant exchange process God has provided for us. When we choose to examine ourselves and allow Him to search the dark recesses of our heart, we begin to work in relationship with God. We give Him liberty to reveal hidden motivations and unhealthy patterns of thinking as He renews our minds. Much of our suffering comes from our lack of knowledge and understanding. There are seasons of brokenness when we are allowed to experience the "valley of the shadow of death" but that is not where God intends us to live. As we submit to our transformation process, we will begin to view life through a new lens and we will walk in effective, productive and more joyful lives.

---

*"Father, I submit myself to Your examination. Search me and reveal to me the hidden motivations of my heart. Help me to recognize and deal with these issues. Forgive me for my fearful and anxious thoughts. I give these thoughts to You at the Cross*

*to be put to death. Renew a right spirit within me Lord. I thank You for Your faithfulness to guide me and to forgive me. I forgive myself for harboring these dark things within my heart and for keeping You from touching them and bringing healing into my life. I want to be whole, Jesus. I don't want to live in fear and anxiety any more. I give you my striving and I thank You for meeting all my needs. Only You, Father, know the real me. Remove the veil from my eyes and let me see Your truth and life."*

## Negative Beliefs

I don't know who I am.
Nothing works for me.
Everything seems to go wrong for me.
How did I lose everything I desired?
I am a failure.
How could anyone love me?
I hate myself.

## Scriptural Truths

I am a child of God.
I am His creation.
God does not make mistakes, so I am not a mistake.
I have a purpose and destiny for my life.
God wants to be my Father.
Old things are now in the past, all things in my life can now become new.
Everything God creates has purpose and beauty.
Conflict is sometimes necessary to guide me to truth.

## Scripture Meditations: "It is written..."

Psalm 139:23-24 — "Search me, O God, and know my heart; try me and know my anxious thoughts; and see if there be any hurtful way in me, and lead me in the everlasting way."

Jeremiah 1:5a — "Before I formed you in the womb I knew you, and before you were born I consecrated you."

Philippians 4:19 — "And my God shall supply all your needs according to His riches in glory in Christ Jesus."

2 Corinthians 3:12,16-18 — "Since we know that this new glory will never go away, we can preach with great boldness, and not as Moses did, who put a veil over his face so that the Israelis could not see the glory fade away.....But whenever anyone turns to the Lord from his sins, then the veil is taken away. The Lord is the Spirit who gives them life, and where He is there is freedom (from trying to be saved by keeping the laws of God).But we have no veil over our faces; we can be mirrors that brightly reflect the glory of the Lord. And as the Spirit of the Lord works within us, we become more and more like him." (Living Bible)

## Reflections...

_____

_____

_____

_____

_____

_____

# 18
# FEAR, ANXIETY AND DEPRESSION

There is a challenging and life-threatening emotion that mankind has battled since time began. Its name is Fear. Like an epidemic, the insidious root of fear has taken hold in society and the Church, sprouting worry, anxiety, depression, physical and emotional illness and more. Fear is contagious and as we succumb to its lies we become infected and transmit it to others. It steals our energy and robs us of joy and productive lives. It is the silent, unmentionable killer of vision, hope and a victorious life.

Fear is a powerful emotion. The Apostle Paul describes fear in 2 Timothy 1:7 as a spirit: "For God has not given us a spirit of fear, but of power, and love and a sound mind." We sometimes feel helpless knowing how to control it. If we do not recognize or acknowledge fear, we can entertain thoughts or responses that cause us to spiral out of control and make poor choices. Even when we do examine our fear and try to overcome it, we may find ourselves fearing the fear, allowing it to grip us even tighter.

Listening to media reports concerning world and economic events can stir fear in our heart. Living or working with fear-producing people can overwhelm us. Fear can manifest as a thought of an unpleasant memory, a feeling of dreaded anticipation, helplessness, confusion or worry. We may be apprehensive about a decision or entertain thoughts like "*I should*", "*What if,*" or "*I ought to.*" As we entertain fear or experience lengthy periods of duress, our bodies may become exhausted or fatigued. The over secretion of hormones to counteract our daily stress and fear can lay a foundation for sickness and disease. Panic attacks, anxiety and phobias can also develop as we attempt to manage the relentless flood of fears such as: fear of failure, fear of death, fear of sickness, fear of rejection, fear of abandonment, fear of being alone, fear of not being in control, fear caused by hurtful memories, fear of the future, fear of pain, fear of not being good enough and fear of not having enough.

We often feel alone in our battle with fear. We ask ourselves, *"How do I handle fear? How do I extract it from my life?"* In my search for the antidote I have arrived at a few conclusions. One, we must choose to identify our fears. Secondly, we must face our fear. In doing so, we can begin to search for the roots that bind us to fear, by examining our unbiblical thoughts or beliefs. Thirdly, we must understand fear lies within us. We may attach our fear to people or situations in our environment, but the real root of fear is found deep within our soul. It is the absence of love. I do not want to sound simplistic, but understanding and receiving the all-encompassing love of God has helped release me from overwhelming panic and dread. 1 John 4:7-21 instructs us concerning God's love. The Apostle John states in verse 8: "the one who does not love does not know God, for God is love." He continues in verse 16b reminding us "God is love, and the one who abides in love abides in God, and God abides in him." If we do not know God or the depth of God's love, we will not have a secure foundation to anchor us when fearful situations approach us. John guides us toward the real antidote for fear as he states in verse 17-18: "...love is perfected with us, that we may have confidence in the day of judgment; because as He is, so also are we in this world. There is no fear in love; but perfect love casts out fear..."

## People Perish Without Hope

People begin to perish when they are without vision or hope. When our vision is cloudy or destroyed, we can move into hopelessness or despair. This is a very dark and lonely place to live. Even after I experienced miracles and supernatural manifestations of God's Spirit in the mid-1990's, from 1998 to 2001, I entered the dark night of my soul. I was now deep into the process of transformation. There were times I would hear: *"It will never happen for you. You will never be whole. You might as well give up. You missed it. You don't deserve it. You're too old now. No one cares about you anymore.*" I was overwhelmed. It never entered my mind that these thoughts were unscriptural.

During these times a dark cloud formed over my mind that would not let me see any truth. I began to agree with these thoughts. I was weary and tired of searching and digging for healing and restoration of my life. I was a mess. I was self-centered and self-serving. The pride and control in me had been revealed. All my good intentions and perceptions of life had been exposed as nothing but waste. All my beliefs were uncovered as self-righteousness. After taking a good look at myself and the problems in my life, I concluded these thoughts bombarding my mind were probably right.

I continued to spiral down into that familiar dark abyss while still trying to keep my job. I loved working with the children in my assigned school. I had worked with children as a Speech-Language Therapist for 28 years. Their smiling faces had always been a highlight of each day. But now I struggled. Paper work overwhelmed me. I felt like I was out of control, trying to hold on with my fingertips. My job and financial provision would soon come to a screeching halt. Fear assaulted me with intense anxiety and depression. I couldn't seem to make my life "work" anymore.

One day, while walking back from lunch to my room, in 1999, I looked down and noticed that it didn't feel like my feet were touching the ground. I remember thinking how strange it felt. By the next afternoon during a parent conference, I began having difficulty breathing. I broke out in perspiration and felt very nauseous. The room began to spin. I held onto the desk in a panic which brought the meeting to an abrupt stop. Everyone at the conference table asked, *"Are you alright?"* I actually didn't know. Once again, I was out of control. I held on to the table trying not to pass out.

My principal encouraged me to call my husband and go home. I had slipped on food left on the cafeteria floor earlier in the morning and thought maybe I had injured myself in the fall. *What could it be?* My husband picked me up and transported me to the doctor for a check up. The medical report stated that I was experiencing vertigo and I exhibited a mild loss of hearing in my left ear. All other vital signs appeared normal. I was given medication to assist with the vertigo and told to rest for a few days. School was only a few days from closing for the summer. I would have the summer to rest and prepare for the next year. I had to get well. *What would I do if I didn't have my job? How would we meet our bills? What would I do if I didn't teach?* I had worked since I was twelve.

The vertigo was relentless. It was not going away. Further testing resulted in a medical diagnosis - Benign Positional Vertigo, which basically meant that in certain positions your vertigo would worsen. Later the diagnosis would change to Meniere's disease, which concerns the inner ear causing the vertigo symptoms. Nothing really changed. I would wake up out of my sleep with the room spinning, grabbing the bed trying to hang on and stop the spins. During the day I felt like my head was floating and bobbing up and down in water. It was difficult to concentrate and with the medications, I found myself sleeping fourteen to sixteen hours a day.

## The Breakdown

My youngest brother came from out of state to visit my parents during the summer. He is a psychologist and was evidently observing my behaviors and symptoms. During the close of one of our visits, he pulled me aside and asked some probing questions. How was I feeling? Did I feel I needed to go back to work this fall? How would I feel if I did not return to work? The questions continued as he gracefully guided me to a revelation that I might not be able to return to work and that I appeared to be exhibiting signs of depression and anxiety. He encouraged me to get a complete examination with another psychologist. It was shocking to think I might be depressed, but what he was sharing somehow made sense. So, I made the appointment and days later received the diagnosis. I was depressed and showed high levels of anxiety. This was a hard pill to swallow. I needed to be well to work and pay my bills and a psychologist was now telling me I was exhibiting depression, and what some would call emotional illness. Well, I saw no choice but to take the medication and begin counseling visits. Obviously something was very wrong. Over the summer, I resigned from my position and decided to try Elementary Counseling. Maybe a fresh start in another school or in another position would lift my spirit. So, I took my antidepressants and forged ahead one more year working and doing all for the glory of God. I was on assignment with a new plan and purpose. I would be strong and try to once again take control of my life.

The year was very busy and difficult. New protocols and job duties loomed before me, as well as a decision to go back and get a second master's degree so I could continue my new position as an Elementary Counselor. I enjoyed being with the students, counseling and evaluating them for special programs and meeting with parents in conferences as we considered placement of their children. It seemed like a good fit. The medications seemed to be working. The vertigo was not as severe. I was sure this was the plan of God. By the end of the school year I was once again, exhausted, confused, and certainly unable to take coursework toward another degree. Reality hit me and I knew I was finished. I would resign from this position and try to stay home. People graciously celebrated my early retirement but I felt empty and afraid. I wasn't ready to quit. I didn't want to give up my financial security and retirement benefits. I didn't want to leave the children.

I realized I did not have any energy to clean my house, let alone work anywhere else. I gave up in defeat. *Now, what in the world was I going to do?* I began to see that I had made my job and career my life. I had learned to value myself by what I was able to accomplish in my work and how much money I was able to make. Now I had neither. In my mind, I had once again failed – more than that –

God had failed me again. In the next few months I experienced an emotional breakdown. I had experienced milder seasons of emotional distress before, but this was the "whole enchilada." From 2000 – 2001, I stayed at home and found comfort and security in my bed. I had little desire to see anyone. The year became a time of rest and reflection; a time to safely and privately begin to examine myself and my thoughts. I was over 50 years old. What had I done with my life and what did I really believe? How strange it was to look at myself and realize I did not really know this person at all. I was a total stranger to myself. I really had no idea anymore who I was, or what I liked or disliked. I would look in the mirror and see a stranger wearing a mask. I began to see that I had lived my life as a chameleon becoming who anyone needed me to be so I would be liked, accepted, loved and valued. And now, I was none of these. I was a void and empty person, living in a dark joyless abyss wondering who I was.

Phone calls to my brother, Scripture, CDs, books and counseling sessions all began to bring little rays of light and truth. I became overwhelmed with the depth of deception in which I had lived; an unhealthy world of misperceptions and skewed motivations. I had pointed the finger at everyone else but never at me. It was not the situations around me or what people had done to me, it was me. The problem was within me. I was responsible for my choices, my perceptions, and my reactions to life around me. I now realized I had the choice to be free.

Even though there is great debate over medications, they were important for my return to health. They gave me rest, proper sleep, combined with enough strength and mental clarity to process the emotional issues that seemed overwhelming. In time, I exited the dark abyss and I no longer needed medication.

Fear is not only an emotion but a spirit. It can be debilitating. Anxiety and depression are very real. Whether they result from traumas in life or chemical imbalance in the brain, they are devastating to everyone involved. Fear can manifest when our basic needs are not being met, or when we have unfulfilled expectations.

Depression involves not only emotional illness, but physical as well. Body aches, muscle spasms and more sinister diseases can result from extended periods of emotional distress. The illnesses are real, but they may develop from emotional roots. The Scripture "be not conformed to this world, but be transformed by the renewing of your mind....." (Romans 12:2) becomes more clear when we begin to understand God truly desires for us to not only walk in physical health but emotional health as well. And as we become more aware of God's profound love, we will begin to experience release and freedom from debilitating fear.

## Negative Beliefs

I must do everything I can to control my life so I may live well.
Working hard will make me happy and successful.
If I have enough money I will be happy.
Happiness comes from who I am, how I look and what I own.
Fear will always control me.

## Scriptural Truths

I may make choices, but God ultimately controls my life and
   destiny.
Happiness and hard work brings only temporary gratification.
Contentment and peace come in a relationship with God.
Materialism and financial gain bring temporal comfort, but deep
   assurance comes by the Spirit of God and His love.
My value is not in what I have, but in who I am in Christ.
God does not desire for us to live in fear.

## Scripture Meditations: "It is written..."

2 Timothy 1:7 — "God has not given me a spirit of fear, but of

power, love and a sound mind."

Psalm 46:1-2 — "God is our refuge and strength, a very present help in trouble. Therefore we will not fear though the earth should change, and though the mountains slip into the heart of the sea."

Isaiah 54:17 — "No weapon that is formed against you will prosper; and every tongue that accuses you in judgment you will condemn. This is the heritage of the servants of the Lord and their vindication is from me."

Psalm 34:15 — "The eyes of the Lord are upon the righteous, and his ears are open to their cry."

John 14:27 — "Peace I leave with you, my peace I give to you: not as the world gives, do I give to you. Let not your heart be troubled, nor let it be fearful."

Proverbs 29:25 — "The fear of man brings a snare: but whoever puts his trust in the Lord shall be safe."

1 John 4:18 — "There is no fear in love; but perfect love casts out fear: because fear involves punishment, and the one who fears is not perfected in love."

Psalm 32:7 — "You are my hiding place; You preserve me from trouble; You surround me with songs of deliverance."

## Reflections...

# 19
# THE PEARL OF GREAT PRICE

As a young girl accepting Christ, my perception of salvation was that once I had Jesus living in me, I had completed my part and now He would do everything else. Scripture told me: "Therefore, if any man is in Christ, he is a new creature: old things are passed away; behold all things become new." I believed I was now perfected and my life would be free from challenges or pain. When life events would turn into hardship, I would become confused and begin to feel rejected and punished by God. I would feel abandoned and alone. What I did not understand was upon accepting Christ I had really stepped into a process of transformation which would work to sanctify the unbelieving, unhealthy parts of my heart. This deep work by Holy Spirit would begin to mature me and change me more into the image of Jesus. "For by one offering He has perfected forever those who are being sanctified" (Hebrews 10:14, NKJV). Upon closer examination of this Scripture the word "being" sanctified was illuminated, which suggested that I was now in a process of change. Was this what they meant when they talked about maturing in Christ?

Apostle Paul's letters to the church of Ephesus began with many accepting Christ. Paul understood the importance of unity and maturing in Christ. By teaching them God's word they also began to have understanding which brought faith and balance. Ephesus became a very stable and mature church. Ephesians 4:13-15 states: "Till we all come to the unity of the faith, and of the knowledge of the Son of God, to a mature man, to the measure of the stature of the fullness of Christ. As a result, we are no longer to be children, tossed to and fro, and carried about with every wind of doctrine, by the trickery of men, by cunning craftiness, whereby they lie in wait to deceive: but speaking the truth in love, we are to grow in all aspects unto Him, which is the head, even Christ" Paul was telling them that God would transform them into the image of Christ in all areas of their lives.

When I accepted Christ, I entered into His covenant, which told me that He would give all of Himself to me, but He would require all of me to be given to Him. My lack of knowing God and understanding His nature, His precepts and statutes set the stage for poor choices and failure. When I began to reap from the poor decisions I had sown, instead of dealing with my own behaviors and actions, I became confused and wondered why God was not around to help me. I ran away from God instead of to Him. I didn't realize God desired to be intimate and communicate with me. The foundations of my beliefs were poorly laid. Jesus spoke to His disciples in Luke 6:46-49 teaching them that if their foundation was laid upon the rock, when the storms or floods came, they would not be shaken. But for those who called Him Lord and chose not to heed what He instructed; their house would be built without any foundation, collapsing when the storms of life came.

Scripture encourages us to seek wisdom and knowledge; however, I looked at God's laws as confining and controlling. It did not occur to me that He gave His statutes in loving concern for my well-being. My belief system was skewed. At times I viewed God as a controller, asking me to make choices I didn't like or want to make. God is not a controller. He has allowed all humanity to make choices. He has given man free will. God is a Father who allows His children freedom. He tries to teach us His laws of the universe so when we make our choices we will live well. But when we, either through lack of knowledge or rebellion, choose to break a universal law or one of His statutes, He must stand by and in His grief watch, as we reap the experience from our actions. Today this is called natural consequences.

Throughout most of my life I strived for perfection and toward the ideal of achieving a successful and idyllic life free from pain and challenges. My dream was to live in my little world of peace and tranquility surrounded by my white picket fence. Life was to bring happiness and joy because I was able to do the things I wanted to do when I wanted to do them. It was important for everyone to be happy and at peace. I heard from the media that the world was to be my oyster and I was digging for the pearl. I would be wonderful, successful, admired and loved, as well as talented, creative and financially prosperous.

## Finding the Pearl

After many years of failed effort, desperately trying to control my life and happiness, as well as making many poor choices, I collapsed in exhaustion. I was unable to make my dreams come true. I came to the realization of my self-centeredness and my inability to achieve anything in my own strength or intellect. This revelation was precious and costly. It was the Pearl of Great Price (Matthew 13:44-46); the Kingdom of heaven. It took a major part of my life to find it. It was a magnificent pearl that ultimately brought healing, rest, joy, and finally peace. This was a pearl I did not have to go looking for – it was offered to me. The price was giving myself to God, giving Him my life to mold and shape as He sees fit, while surrendering my control and intellectual knowledge of what I think is best. It included my acceptance of God's dealings with me as good, trusting Him above all. No matter how I strived or struggled trying to run away from the very Creator that could show me real life; I would always return to the One who unconditionally loved me, Jesus.

There was a price to pay just as Jesus paid a price for us – the Cross. I began to understand the reality of His covenant and that as He gave all of Himself to me, He was expecting all of me to be given to Him. As Scripture states, we perish for our lack of knowledge and understanding. I finally understood, my life was not my own.

My lack of Biblical understanding as well as the ungodly beliefs I entertained as truth and reality, kept me from health, joy and peace for many years. My misperceptions of God and the world around me caused me to take on years of striving for acceptance, while carrying false responsibilities and burdens. I needed to validate my existence and my right to be living. Guilt and shame coupled with pride and self-importance accompanied me daily taking on various forms and disguises. Dark periods in my life often brought confusion and despair. *Why was I having so much difficulty being healed? Why wouldn't the pain leave? Where was the elusive peace and love I so desperately desired? Why was I never able to feel rested or content? Why did life have to be so difficult and so challenging? Where was God while I was hurting and feeling alone? Why does God not answer my prayers?* Unanswered prayer can take a toll on us spiritually. We are reminded in Proverbs 13:12, "Hope deferred makes the heart sick: but desire fulfilled is a tree of life."

I still don't have the answer to why my prayers sometime seem to go unanswered, but I have come to realize that either God will answer me, or in His wisdom He is waiting on the appropriate season or timing of release. There also may be some things hidden that He is working on and the answer will come later. I do know when the answer does finally come, it is a tree of life that brings joy and we can jump up and down rejoicing as in Isaiah 25:9: "And it shall be said in that day, Behold, this is our God for whom we have waited that He might save us. This is the Lord for whom we have waited; Let us rejoice and be glad in His salvation." God does not want us to lose heart. He encourages us to keep knocking, keep searching, and waiting, as He develops perseverance and endurance within us.

Through continued counsel and prayer, I now see the dark seasons of my life actually have given me great gifts. We previously discussed Isaiah 45:3, but let's be reminded one more time of this precious promise. "I will give you the treasures hidden in the darkness, secret riches; and you will know that I am doing this — I, the Lord, the God of Israel, the One who calls you by your name." (Living Bible) The greatest gift we receive from God during dark periods in our life is the opportunity to know Him more intimately as our Lord. We discover He truly knows our name and identifies with our sorrow.

Challenges and obstacles often bring fear and pain. In those times it is very difficult for us to see that any good can come out of our great darkness and despair. It can be difficult to believe God loves us and has our best interest in His heart. Nevertheless, when life seems dark, even though it is not always easy, we can learn to look for the treasure and revelation God desires to give us. He will give life-changing keys and truths if we ask.

## Embracing Transformation

When we are completely emptied and at the end of ourselves and we understand God's plan for our own redemption, then He can truly reveal His glorious faithfulness and mercy to us. In our search for answers and resolution we find Him, the magnificent Pearl. He desires to reveal His nature and character to us, and we seem to look and listen more attentively in our valleys. When we encounter our greatest needs, we begin to know and trust Him as Jehovah-Jireh, our provider and supplier. When we become unlovable, we receive His amazing and unconditional love and see Him as Jehovah-Shalom, our peace and prosperity. When we feel alone and forsaken, we begin to understand and sense His presence that is ever with us as He reveals Himself as Jehovah-Shammah. When we are cast into great despair, we begin to experience the impact of His life-sustaining joy as He comforts us as our Shepherd, Jehovah-Rohi. God is a Restorer who brings redemption and reconciliation to His children. In Jeremiah 30:17, He once again shares His love and desire to see us healed and whole: "For I will restore health unto you, and I will heal you of your wounds, says the Lord; because they called you an outcast, saying: 'It is Zion, no one cares for her.'"

When Paul wrote to the brethren in Philippi, his main theme was to teach them of the all-sufficiency of Christ that was continually present and always working in every part of their lives, whether they encountered good or bad times. He encouraged them in Philippians chapter 2, verse 12, to ".... work out your own salvation with fear and trembling." The book of Philippians gives wonderful instruction in the importance of experiencing love and joy, as we are united in Spirit by God developing our character and integrity. Daily, Holy Spirit is at work conforming us into the image of Christ, developing humility and obedience, teaching us how to embrace the Cross while we gain the understanding that "God is at work in you both to will and to work for His good pleasure." (verse 13) Paul also conveyed his revelation in chapter 1, verse 20-21, that he could now conclude Christ is the significance of life and death: "According to my earnest expectation and hope, that I shall not be put to shame in anything, but that with all boldness, Christ shall even now, as always, be exalted in my body, whether by life or by death. For to me, to live is Christ, and to die is gain."

The greater the sorrow we experience, the greater the capacity for joy in our lives. When we experience adversity, little things in the world become more cherished and savored. Life is not so easily taken for granted. The fresh breeze that touches our face becomes a kiss from God, and the fragrance of jasmine causes us to pause and breathe in its beauty. The phone call from a friend becomes a cherished gift as we are awakened to the importance of relationships and love. A turquoise dragonfly suspended in flight brings a smile as he poses, as if greeting me and wishing me a good day. Seemingly unimportant things we once overlooked or took for granted now become daily treasures from God.

## A Roadmap for Transformation

Any journey is made easier with the help of a roadmap. In asking God for understanding He directed me to The Beatitudes in Matthew 5:3-12. I believe these Scriptures included in The Sermon on the Mount, are a roadmap to help us identify where we are in our journey of transformation. When we accept Jesus to live within us, we begin a covenant journey of God exchanging our nature for His nature. As we surrender to God, we enter a progressive process where He desires to take all of who we are and He gives us all of Him. What a deal! He begins to exchange our character for His character; our nature and integrity for His nature and integrity. God's goal is to make us look more like Jesus. This is a process that can take us by surprise, often with twists and turns, shock and even pain. When the winds of adversity blow, the enemy is often the source of our challenges and trials; but in those hard places God gives us an opportunity to be changed and conformed to His image, to be blessed, enlarged and satisfied.

The life of Jesus is a prophetic image of the Beatitudes. He shared this poignant and sobering sermon and then He walked through every verse to show us the way to God's Kingdom. His message encourages us that we are blessed on "account of Him" (verse 11). Blessed (makarios) is to be characterized by the quality of God. In other words, when God dwells within us with His nature, we are able to experience His Kingdom and so we are blessed. Blessed also means to be fully satisfied; not due to any reward or fulfillment we experience, but we are satisfied because Jesus lives within us. We learn to walk through adversity and trials basically satisfied because we know that Christ and God's Kingdom dwell within our heart.

As challenging trials and testing occur, it is always comforting to visit the Beatitudes, where I become aware of the surgery Holy Spirit is performing in me concerning my exchange process. When we see how God is working to bless us in our circumstances and mature us into His image, peace is restored. The process of covenant exchange is a divine work orchestrated by Holy Spirit.

*"Blessed are the poor in spirit, for theirs is the kingdom of heaven"* (Matthew 5:3).

One of the first stops we will encounter on our transforming journey is to recognize how spiritually helpless we are without

God. When we understand that we are unable to make anything of ourselves, we then become blessed or fully satisfied. Jesus shared that He only did what He saw the Father doing. Jesus was saying *"You are fully satisfied when you realize your spiritual helplessness, and that you can not make more out of yourself."* We gain new depth and revelation into Jesus as the captain of our salvation, as well as God's stunning grace and mercy.

---

*"Blessed are those who mourn, for they shall be comforted"* *(verse 4).*

---

In Gethsemane, Jesus mourned, identifying with our hopelessness and our helplessness. He showed us how to surrender to God, when we recognize that we can't make any more of ourselves. Mourn (hoi pentheō) is the sorrow we experience from our sin and the sins of others. We become faced with our own humanity. When we begin to see and mourn our hopelessness and the futility in trying to change ourselves, we then become blessed, and God comforts and encourages us. The Kingdom becomes manifest, and we become satisfied. His great love and comfort becomes tangible to us. We begin to marvel at His extravagant and amazing love that turns our mourning into dancing (Psalm 30:11-12).

---

*"Blessed are the meek for they shall inherit the earth"* *(verse 5).*

---

As we experience situations where we are humbled or made meek, we learn to yield to God. Meekness can be defined as "accepting God's dealings with us as 'good,' without disputing, contending or resisting." Throughout scriptures Jesus experienced persecution, betrayal, rejection, abuse, slander and great humiliation. He became a living model of the character of meekness and humility that God desires to impart to us. Jesus continually surrendered

Himself to God's will. When we learn to accept God's dealings with us without anger or contentiousness, God is able to bless and enlarge us. He gives us strength as He releases His healing virtue to overcome pain in our soul and teaches us humility.

---

*"Blessed are they which do hunger and thirst for righteousness, for they shall be satisfied" (verse 6).*

---

When we hunger and thirst after God, we are famished and in need of constant refueling with the righteousness and essence of God. We choose to surrender to His laws and commands; we conform to His desires and will, and then He fills us and satisfies us. We become content, peaceful and fulfilled. Jesus always revealed God's righteousness. He became the image on earth of the nature and character of God.

---

*"Blessed are the merciful for they shall obtain mercy" (verse 7).*

---

We will experience situations when we will be challenged to extend mercy. Mercy involves thought and action. God is the one who gives strength for grace as He requests that we extend mercy to avoid sin. Jesus exhibited active compassion when He saved the woman's life by asking "You who has not sinned — throw the first stone." (John 8:7). He moved with compassion and touched many. He demonstrated for us how to pardon others by God's grace. So when we find ourselves in a circumstance to choose revenge or to extend mercy, we become blessed when we choose mercy and obtain God's mercy for ourselves. We learn the importance of forgiveness and how to love our enemies and pray for those who have persecuted us. We begin to see God's creation through His eyes and His love.

*"Blessed are the pure in heart for they shall see God" (verse 8).*

Becoming pure in heart is a process of purification or continual cleansing. This process by Holy Spirit frees us from negative things residing in our heart, our thoughts, emotions and paradigms. As we begin to surrender to His covenant exchange, we are blessed and are able to behold God with clearer vision. We are able to gaze upon His beauty with greater clarity. The blood of Christ becomes more real to us as He enlarges our understanding of His cleansing blood that purifies us. Our past, no longer defines us and we begin to see ourselves as His beloved. He takes our old heart; He purifies it (katharos) and cleanses it from the toxins of sin and guilt.

*"Blessed are the peacemakers for they shall be called the children of God" (verse 9).*

We do not become blessed simply by making peace between two parties. Peacemaker in this context is one who is able to make peace in others, because he has first received the peace of God in his own heart. So we are fully satisfied and blessed as we receive His love and covenant of peace. We begin to understand the Cross as we identify with the violence Christ suffered. We see clearly how His suffering canceled the enemy's power forever. We begin to experience God's peace and are then prepared to extend it to others.

*"Blessed are those who have been persecuted for the sake of righteousness, for theirs is the kingdom of heaven" (verse 10). "Blessed are you when men cast insults at you, and persecute you and say all kinds of evil against you falsely, on account of Me" (verse 11). "Rejoice and be glad for your reward in heaven is great, for so they persecuted the prophets who were before you" (verse 12).*

As we begin to walk in God's righteousness or His revealed will, false accusations, rejection, reproach, defamation and taunting will occur. We begin to identify with Christ's sufferings and the rejection, betrayal, and false accusations He endured. God's Kingdom becomes more manifest in us as we begin to respond with His nature, extending love, grace, mercy, and forgiveness instead of our old nature of disappointment, bitterness, anger or revenge.

His Kingdom emerges from within us and we become carriers of His love and presence. We begin to experience the life of His Spirit. We grow in His grace, wisdom, power and might. We see and hear more clearly into the heavenly realm, as we begin to experience our rewards (misthos) here on earth as well as those being established in heaven. The eyes of our understanding open to greater depth and revelation of His Kingdom and life.

God's covenant exchange is a lifetime process. We may walk through the Beatitudes cyclically as God deals with us. First, we are faced with a challenge we cannot change. We begin to understand we are unable to make anything out of ourselves. We then begin to mourn, because we see our sin and helplessness. We become humbled in our weakness and begin to hunger for His righteousness and revealed will, knowing He is the only one who can save us. We gain insight of His grace and begin to develop mercy that we choose to extend to others making us more Christ-like. Our heart becomes purified in this situation. We obtain His peace and are then able to share that peace with others. We learn to bless, forgive, encourage and love as we face persecution. We receive more of the nature of God and His Kingdom expands. New challenges present themselves and we begin the journey again.

As we live out our daily experiences, Holy Spirit is working to change us more into Christ's likeness. When challenges attempt to overtake us, we can learn to rest in His love being assured that all is well. God has given us a roadmap to identify the points of our transformation process. And as we travel with Him on this amazing and progressive journey, He will continue to exchange

His nature with us, establishing His Kingdom and Covenant.

## God Desires Relationship

God desires for us to know Him and to understand He is a God of love who takes every opportunity to reveal Himself and His nature to His creation. His names declare who He is: Master, Lord, Possessor of Heaven and Earth, Supplier, Sanctifier, Conqueror, Shepherd, Healer, Peace and Prosperity, Righteousness, Merciful, Good and Just, Redeemer, Restorer, Deliverer, Rock, Tree of Life, Living Water, Gentle and Lowly in Heart, Intercessor, Faithful, Savior, Gracious and Full of Compassion and so many more.

As you continue forward on your journey toward health and wholeness, please be encouraged by the words of Jesus: "Ask, and you will be given what you ask for. Seek, and you will find. Knock, and the door will be opened. For everyone who asks, receives. Anyone who seeks finds. If only you will knock, the door will open. If a child asks his father for a loaf of bread, will he be given a stone instead? If he asks for fish, will he be given a poisonous snake? Of course not! And if you hardhearted, sinful men know how to give good gifts to your children, won't your Father in heaven even more certainly give good gifts to those who ask him for them?" (Matthew 7:7-11, The Living Bible).

The answer to what we ask for may not always come in the way we expect; but in the challenges we face, we will find a merciful and loving Father who desires to guide and comfort us throughout our journey. He will give us precious treasures prepared just for us, intimately and individually wrapped by Him. These treasures will bring insight and guidance to help us live life as well as prepare us for our heavenly home. Jesus comforts us with His promise, in John 14:18, "I will not abandon you or leave you as orphans in the storm: I will come to you." We can experience rest and peace as we trust in this promise that He will not leave us comfortless and He will always be with us.

Beloved, as you continue your journey toward healing and

transformation, may you embrace the pain as you embrace Him. Ask God for wisdom and guidance as you search for the truth that will bring you wholeness and freedom. Watch for Him as He illuminates your path to gain knowledge and understanding. Meditate on His Word and keep His promises before your eyes and in your heart. Talk to God and let Him know your concerns and your fears. Look for His revealed will and direction. Learn to forgive others, as you learn to forgive yourself. Receive His love and comfort and know that He is always near and ever faithful. As you surrender your life, He will perform a divine work as He heals you "inside-out." Above all, you will find the Pearl of Great Price, the Kingdom of Heaven, and a compassionate and loving God. He will graciously and faithfully fill the hole in your heart, as He teaches you that your real hope and life ultimately lies in Him.

## Negative Beliefs

I will never be successful or acceptable.
Mistakes are terrible and irreversible.
What if....?
I should ....
I ought to....
If I had only....
Why didn't I see...?

## Scriptural Truths

Unrealistic and unreachable goals put me in a state of stress causing health problems.
God will give us keys for living as we ask Him for revelation.
Answers to our prayers often come in ways we do not expect.
Ungodly beliefs can keep us from health and happiness.
God teaches us patience and endurance as we navigate through trials and discouragement.

Our pain can lead us to a more intimate relationship with God. True resurrection life comes when I begin to understand the gift of the Cross and God's love and sacrifice for me.

## Scripture Meditations: "It is written..."

Romans 15:13 — "I pray that God who gives you hope will keep you happy and full of peace as you believe in Him. I pray that God will help you overflow with hope in Him through the Holy Spirit's power within you."

Psalm 43:5 — "O, my soul, why be so gloomy and discouraged? Trust in God! I shall again praise him for his wondrous help; he will make me smile again, for he is my God!"

Isaiah 33:6 — "And He shall be the stability of your times, a wealth of salvation: the fear of the Lord is his treasure."

2 Corinthians 1:3-5 — "Blessed be the God and Father of our Lord Jesus Christ, the Father of mercies and God of all comfort; who comforts us in all our affliction so that we may be able to comfort those who are in any affliction, with the comfort with which we ourselves are comforted by God. For just as the sufferings of Christ are ours in abundance, so also our comfort is abundant through Christ."

Matthew 13:45-46 — "Again, the Kingdom of heaven is like a merchant seeking fine pearls, and upon finding one pearl of great value, he went and sold all that he had and bought it."

## Reflections...

# Notes

1       Scriptures compiled from web devotions by Dr. Neil Anderson, Freedom in Christ Ministries, http://www.ficm.org.

2       Zodhiates, Spiros, Th. D. *The Hebrew-Greek Key Study Bible, New American Standard*, (Chattanooga: AMG Publishers, 1977), 1632-1633.

3       Strong, James, *Strong's Exhaustive Concordance*, (Gordonsville, TN: Dugan Publishers, Inc.), Number 3640, 51.

4       Dr. Tom Corbitt and Dr. Dee Corbitt have been our personal nutritionists for many years. Dr. Tom Corbitt is a Master Herbalist, Naturopathic Doctor, and Certified Clinical Nutritionist licensed by the State of Florida Department of Medicine to counsel people on their nutritional needs. Source: http://www.nothinbutherbs.com.

5       Healed of terminal brain cancer at the age of nine, Pastor Billy Burke conducts healing crusades throughout the world. The Billy Burke World Outreach Center is located in Tampa, Florida. Source: http://www.billyburke.org.

6       Randi and Cathy Lechner: Covenant Ministries, Miami, Florida.

7       Barbie Breathitt: Breath of the Spirit Ministries, North Richland, Texas. Source: http://www.breathofthespiritministries.com.

8       Derek Prince was born in India of British parents. He was

educated as a scholar of Greek and Latin at Eton College and Cambridge University, England. He also studied Hebrew and Aramaic, both at Cambridge University and the Hebrew University in Jerusalem. Source: Derek Prince Ministries, http://www.derekprince.org.

9    Dr. Dick Mills: Dick Mills Ministries, Orange, California. Source: http://www.dmm.org.

10   John and Paula Sanford, *Transformation of the Inner Man* (Tulsa: Victory House, 1982). Source: http://www.elijahhouse.org.

11   Nancy Honeytree and Steve Millikan, "Tell Me What Love Is" (Greentree Records, The Benson Company, Inc. Nashville, 1985).

12   W.E. Vine, *Vine's Expository Dictionary of New Testament Words – Unabridged Edition* (Virginia: McDonald Publishing Company), 702-703.

13   Candace Pert, *Molecules of Emotion* (UK: Simon and Schuster, 1997).

14   Dr. Caroline Leaf, *Who Switched Off My Brain?* (Dallas: Switch On Your Brain USA, Inc., 2008), 7.

15   Dr. Caroline Leaf, *Who Switched Off My Brain?* (Dallas: Switch On Your Brain USA, Inc., 2008), 5.

16   Dr. Caroline Leaf, *Who Switched Off My Brain?* (Dallas: Switch On Your Brain USA, Inc., 2008), 4, 70, 74-76, 81-82.

17   John E. Sarno, M.D., *The Divided Mind: The Epidemic of Mindbody Disorders* (New York: Harper Collins Publishers, 2006).

18   Dr. Caroline Leaf, *Who Switched Off My Brain?* (Dallas: Switch On Your Brain USA, Inc., 2008), 107-108.

19   Dr. Caroline Leaf, *Who Switched Off My Brain?* (Dallas: Switch On Your Brain USA, Inc., 2008), 108-109.

20   David Devenish. *Demolishing Strongholds: Effective Strategies for Spiritual Warfare* (UK: Word Publishing, 2000).

21   Dr. Lawrence J. Crabb, Jr., *Effective Biblical Counseling,* (Grand Rapids: Zondervan Publishing, Ministry Resources Library, 1977), 134.

# Biography

Born in Kentucky and raised in Southern Indiana, Rebecca gave her heart to the Lord at four years of age. She attended Ball State University in Muncie, Indiana and received a B.S. degree in Speech Pathology and Library Science. She earned a Master's Degree in Exceptional Student Education from St. Francis University in Ft. Wayne, Indiana. In 1970, she was a Miss Indiana finalist and Ball State University Homecoming Queen.

Rebecca worked in public education for 28 years as a Speech Language Therapist, Special Education Teacher and Librarian. During her educational career, she was honored twice as Teacher of the Year and was recognized as a finalist for Polk County Florida Teacher of the Year.

She has served in children and youth ministry, choir and psalmistry, conducted seminars and taught various classes about God's love, marriage and relationships, prayer and intercession, physical and emotional healing, the gifts of the Spirit and hearing God over the last 35 years. Rebecca is a graduate of King's Way School of Theology in Dayton, Ohio and an ordained minister with training in pastoral counseling.

Rebecca has developed and facilitated numerous home groups with her husband, Richard Maisenbacher. Rebecca and Richard are actively involved in training, equipping, raising up and releasing leaders in the Body of Christ as founders and pastors of The Covenant Center in Lakeland, Florida.

Rebecca shares a transparent message of God's love, forgiveness and redemption that brings healing and peace to others. Her testimony of the ways God transforms His children gives encouragement and faith to those seeking God's healing of physical and emotional pain.

**the Covenant center publishing house**

Founded in 2009, Covenant Publishing House facilitates publishing projects for writers, artists, musicians and teachers associated with The Covenant Center in Lakeland, Florida.

The Covenant Center was birthed from a vision given to Richard and Rebecca Maisenbacher that encompasses individuals and groups from various Christian denominations. We believe that the entire Body of Christ is commissioned to go into the world and make disciples.

The ministry vision is to see the Body of Christ strengthened, equipped and restored through emotional, physical and spiritual healing; and to be an expression of worship through the Creative Arts. The Covenant Center's hope is to encourage and train Saints to minister in their gifts and callings - in the community, marketplace, country and throughout the world, sharing the love of Christ.

For further information, and to find other projects of Covenant Publishing House, please contact:

The Covenant Center Publishing House
26 Lake Wire Drive
PO Box 524
Lakeland, Fl. 33802-0524
www.thecovenantcenter.com
info@thecovenantcenter.com

www.ingramcontent.com/pod-product-compliance
Lightning Source LLC
Chambersburg PA
CBHW071956040426
42447CB00009B/1358